DYLAN FOX

Python Development With AWS lambda

Contents

Introduction to AWS Lambda

hat is AWS Lambda?

W AWS Lambda is a serverless computing service provided by Amazon Web Services (AWS) that allows you to run code without the need to manage servers. It automatically executes code in response to events or triggers, such as changes to data in an S3 bucket, an HTTP request via API Gateway, or a new entry in a DynamoDB table. Lambda takes care of provisioning and managing the backend infrastructure, scaling as needed, and charging you only for the compute time used.

Benefits of Serverless Computing

1. **No Server Management:** With AWS Lambda, you don't need to worry about provisioning, patching, or managing servers. The entire backend infrastructure is abstracted away, allowing developers to focus purely on the application code.

2. **Automatic Scaling:** Lambda automatically scales based on the number of incoming requests or events. It adjusts the number of function invocations concurrently without any manual intervention.

3. **Cost Efficiency:** You are only charged for the compute time that your code consumes. There are no costs for idle resources. This is particularly beneficial for applications with variable or low traffic, as you're not paying for unused capacity.

4. **High Availability:** AWS Lambda is designed to provide high availability

and fault tolerance across multiple Availability Zones (AZs) in an AWS Region, ensuring that your application remains operational even in case of localized failures.

5. **Event-Driven Execution:** Lambda functions can be automatically triggered by a wide range of AWS services, allowing you to build highly reactive, event-driven architectures. This makes it an ideal choice for microservices, automation tasks, and real-time data processing.

Key Concepts: Functions, Triggers, and Events

1. **Functions:** A function in AWS Lambda is essentially your application logic, written in supported programming languages such as Python, Node.js, Java, and more. You upload your function's code, and Lambda takes care of executing it when triggered.

2. **Triggers:** Triggers are the services or conditions that cause a Lambda function to run. Common triggers include changes to objects in S3, new messages in SQS, API requests from API Gateway, or even scheduled executions using CloudWatch Events.

3. **Events:** An event is the input data passed to the Lambda function. This could be anything from the contents of an uploaded file in S3 to an HTTP request's payload. Lambda processes this event and returns the corresponding output. Understanding how to handle events properly is key to leveraging Lambda's power in building efficient workflows.

When to Use AWS Lambda

AWS Lambda is best suited for specific use cases where you want to leverage event-driven, scalable, and cost-effective computing solutions. Some common scenarios include:

- **Real-Time File Processing:** Automatically process uploaded images, videos, or documents in Amazon S3 (e.g., image resizing, transcoding).
- **Data Transformation and ETL:** Streamline and automate ETL pipelines for data lakes by processing streaming data from services like Kinesis or

DynamoDB.

- **Building Microservices:** Use Lambda to create backend services for web and mobile applications, typically connected via API Gateway, without worrying about scaling or infrastructure management.
- **Scheduled Tasks:** Execute code at scheduled intervals using CloudWatch Events or EventBridge for tasks like cleaning up old data, performing backups, or triggering reports.
- **Real-Time Notifications and Alerts:** Process events and send notifications or alerts in real-time, such as sending emails via SES when a specific condition is met in your application.

Getting Started with AWS Lambda and Python

Setting Up an AWS Account

To use AWS Lambda, you first need an active AWS account. Follow these steps to set one up:

1. **Visit the AWS Website:** Go to aws.amazon.com and click on "Create an AWS Account."
2. **Provide Account Information:** You'll need to enter your email address, password, and select a unique AWS account name.
3. **Payment Information:** AWS requires valid payment information, even though many of its services, including Lambda, have free tiers.
4. **Identity Verification:** Complete the verification process by providing your mobile number and verifying it through a code sent to your phone.
5. **Choose a Support Plan:** AWS offers several support plans. The "Basic" plan is free and sufficient for most users starting with Lambda.
6. **Sign In:** After completing registration, you can sign in to the AWS Management Console using your email and password.

Overview of the AWS Management Console

The **AWS Management Console** is a web-based interface where you can manage all AWS services, including AWS Lambda. Here's a brief guide to navigating the console for Lambda:

1. **Dashboard:** Once logged in, the console home page provides quick access to frequently used services. You can search for "Lambda" in the search bar to locate it.
2. **Lambda Dashboard:** The Lambda console allows you to create, manage, and monitor Lambda functions. Key sections include:

- **Functions:** View, create, and manage your Lambda functions.
- **Layers:** Add shared libraries (like Python dependencies) across multiple functions.
- **Event Sources:** Set up triggers for your Lambda function (e.g., API Gateway, S3, DynamoDB).
- **Logs:** Access AWS CloudWatch logs for monitoring and troubleshooting.

1. **Navigation Tools:** The top navigation bar allows you to switch between different AWS regions, view billing, and access documentation.

Installing AWS CLI

The **AWS Command Line Interface (CLI)** is a powerful tool that lets you manage AWS services, including Lambda, from your terminal or command prompt. Here's how to install and set it up:

1. **Install the AWS CLI:**

- **Windows:** Download and install the Windows MSI installer from AWS CLI installation page.
- **Mac/Linux:** Use the following command in your terminal:

```bash
Copy code
```

```
curl "https://awscli.amazonaws.com/AWSCLIV2.pkg"
-o "AWSCLIV2.pkg"
sudo installer -pkg AWSCLIV2.pkg -target /
```

- Alternatively, you can use Homebrew on macOS:

```bash
bash
Copy code
brew install awscli
```

1. **Verify the Installation:** To confirm that the AWS CLI is installed, type the following command in your terminal:

```bash
bash
Copy code
aws --version
```

1. You should see the version of the CLI that is installed.
2. **Configure the AWS CLI:** Run the following command to configure your credentials:

```bash
bash
Copy code
aws configure
```

1. You'll be prompted to enter:

- **AWS Access Key ID:** Obtain this from the AWS Management Console by creating a new IAM user.
- **AWS Secret Access Key:** Also obtained when setting up IAM user credentials.
- **Default Region Name:** Enter the region closest to you (e.g., us-east-1 or eu-west-1).
- **Default Output Format:** You can select either json, text, or table. The most common format is json.

Creating Your First Lambda Function with Python

1. **Go to AWS Lambda Console:**

- Navigate to the AWS Lambda section from the Management Console. Click on **"Create function"**.

1. **Choose a Function Blueprint:**

- Choose **"Author from scratch"** to create a basic function. Provide a name (e.g., HelloWorldPython) and select **Python 3.8** or a newer version as the runtime.
- For the **Execution Role**, choose **"Create a new role with basic Lambda permissions"**. This will automatically generate the necessary permissions to access CloudWatch logs.

1. **Write Your Lambda Function Code:**

- You'll see a code editor on the console. Replace the default code with a simple Python function:

```python
Copy code
def lambda_handler(event, context):
    return {
        'statusCode': 200,
        'body': 'Hello from AWS Lambda!'
    }
```

- This function takes in an event and context (standard in AWS Lambda functions) and returns a simple message.

1. **Configure the Function:**

- **Memory and Timeout Settings:** You can adjust the memory and maximum execution time for your function. The default settings (128 MB of memory and a 3-second timeout) are usually sufficient for simple tasks.
- **Environment Variables:** If your function needs specific configurations, you can add environment variables here (e.g., API keys or database connection strings).

1. **Set Up a Trigger:**

- You can configure a trigger from several AWS services like API Gateway, S3, or DynamoDB. For this example, you can create an **API Gateway** trigger by selecting "API Gateway" as the source and choosing "**HTTP API**".
- This will create a publicly accessible API endpoint that triggers your Lambda function.

1. **Test Your Function:**

- Once the function is set up, you can test it directly from the console.

Click **"Test"** and configure a test event by choosing a template like "API Gateway Proxy."

- Click **"Test"** to run the function, and you should see a 200 status code response along with your message: 'Hello from AWS Lambda!'

1. **Deploy and Invoke Your Function:**

- After testing, click **"Deploy"** to make your function live. You can now invoke the function using its API Gateway URL or by creating other event triggers like uploading a file to S3 or adding a new DynamoDB record.

Understanding the Lambda Execution Model

How Lambda Functions Work

AWS Lambda operates on a serverless execution model, meaning that developers only need to write the function logic, and AWS handles the underlying infrastructure.

- **Function Invocation:** A Lambda function is invoked in response to an event or trigger. AWS Lambda receives the event, executes the function with the event as input, and returns a result.
- **Stateless Nature:** Lambda functions are stateless, which means they don't maintain any state between invocations. If your function requires state, it must retrieve it from external sources such as databases or object storage.
- **Containers:** AWS Lambda runs your function inside lightweight, isolated containers. Each container runs a specific function version with its runtime environment, such as Python, Node.js, or Java.
- **Execution Flow:**

1. An event source (e.g., S3, API Gateway, or a scheduled CloudWatch Event) triggers the function.
2. The function is executed within the container.

3. The output is returned to the event source or a specified destination.
4. If needed, AWS Lambda terminates the container when it's idle.

Event Sources and Triggers

An **event source** is any service or application that generates events, which can invoke a Lambda function. **Triggers** are configurations that link an event source to the Lambda function. Common event sources include:

- **Amazon S3:** Lambda can automatically invoke a function in response to object uploads, deletions, or modifications in an S3 bucket. For example, resizing an image or processing log files.
- **Amazon DynamoDB:** You can configure Lambda to respond to changes in a DynamoDB table, such as inserting, updating, or deleting records. This is useful for data replication or event-driven architectures.
- **Amazon API Gateway:** Lambda can be triggered by HTTP requests made through API Gateway, allowing you to build serverless REST APIs or backends.
- **Amazon SNS/SQS:** Lambda functions can process messages from Simple Notification Service (SNS) or Simple Queue Service (SQS) to handle event-driven workflows or background processing.
- **CloudWatch Events and EventBridge:** These allow for scheduled or event-driven execution of Lambda functions. For instance, you can run a function every night to process logs or data.

Lambda Limits and Quotas

Lambda comes with specific limits and quotas to ensure efficient operation and resource management. Here are some key limitations:

1. **Execution Time (Timeout):** A Lambda function can run for a maximum of **15 minutes** per invocation. You must ensure that your code completes within this period, or the function will be automatically terminated.
2. **Memory and CPU Allocation:** Lambda functions can be allocated

between **128 MB to 10 GB** of memory. The amount of CPU power available scales with the memory setting, so more memory also increases the CPU resources.

3. **Request and Response Payload Size:**

- **Request Payload (Event Input):** Up to **6 MB** of request payload can be passed to the function.
- **Response Payload:** The response output size is limited to **6 MB** for synchronous invocations and **256 KB** for asynchronous invocations.

1. **Concurrency Limits:** AWS Lambda limits the number of concurrent function executions. By default, there's a soft limit of **1,000 concurrent executions** per account in a region, but you can request a higher limit.
2. **Deployment Package Size:**

- **Compressed Deployment Package:** The size of the .zip file uploaded directly is limited to **50 MB**.
- **Uncompressed Package:** Once deployed, the uncompressed size can be up to **250 MB**.

1. **Environment Variables:** AWS Lambda allows up to **4 KB** of environment variable data for configuring your function with runtime settings.

Understanding these limits is essential when designing scalable and efficient Lambda functions, as you may need to split work into smaller invocations, manage concurrency, or optimize code for size.

Cold Starts and Warm Invocations

Lambda functions are run in isolated environments, and the way these environments are managed impacts performance. Lambda functions experience either **cold starts** or **warm invocations** depending on the container's lifecycle:

- **Cold Starts:**

- A cold start happens when AWS Lambda invokes your function for the first time or after a period of inactivity. In this case, AWS must allocate a new container, download your function code, and initialize the environment. This process can introduce a delay (sometimes several hundred milliseconds or more), especially in functions with large dependencies or complex initialization code.
- Key factors affecting cold starts:
- **Runtime:** Some runtimes, such as Java or .NET, tend to have longer cold start times compared to Python or Node.js.
- **Function Size:** Large deployment packages or functions with complex initialization processes can increase cold start times.
- **Memory Allocation:** Functions with more memory tend to experience faster cold starts because they have more CPU resources allocated.
- **Warm Invocations:**
- If a function is invoked repeatedly within a short time frame, AWS reuses the existing container to execute the function, known as a **warm invocation**. These invocations are faster since the environment is already initialized, significantly reducing latency.
- Warm invocations are common in functions with high traffic or those that run frequently. However, if there's a period of inactivity, AWS may deallocate the container, leading to another cold start when the function is invoked again.

Mitigating Cold Starts:

- **Provisioned Concurrency:** AWS offers a feature called **Provisioned Concurrency** to reduce cold start latency. You can pre-allocate a certain number of containers that are always "warm" and ready to handle requests, ensuring consistent performance.
- **Code Optimization:** Minimizing the initialization time in your code, using fewer dependencies, and keeping the function lightweight can reduce cold start delays.

Understanding the Lambda Execution Model

How Lambda Functions Work

AWS Lambda operates as an event-driven, serverless compute service. It runs your code in response to triggers or events, allowing you to focus on writing the logic without managing servers. Here's how the Lambda execution process works:

1. **Function Creation:** You write and upload a function in supported languages (e.g., Python, Node.js, Java).

2. **Event Trigger:** An event (such as an HTTP request, file upload to S3, or database modification) triggers the Lambda function.

3. **Execution:** AWS Lambda runs your function in a managed environment that includes the necessary runtime and libraries. The function is executed inside an isolated container.

4. **Event Input and Context:** Lambda provides the event data and execution context to your function, allowing it to process the incoming data.

5. **Result:** The function processes the event and returns a result to the triggering service or destination (e.g., API Gateway, S3).

6. **Scaling:** Lambda automatically scales with the number of incoming requests. AWS provisions more containers as needed without manual

intervention.

Lambda's stateless nature means that each invocation is independent, and any data that needs to persist between invocations must be stored externally, such as in a database or object storage.

Event Sources and Triggers

Lambda can be triggered by a wide range of AWS services and external events. Some common **event sources** include:

1. **Amazon S3:** Automatically triggers a function when objects are uploaded, modified, or deleted in an S3 bucket (e.g., image processing after an upload).
2. **Amazon DynamoDB:** Invokes Lambda when records in a DynamoDB table are inserted, updated, or deleted (useful for real-time analytics or processing change logs).
3. **Amazon API Gateway:** Allows HTTP(S) requests to trigger Lambda, which is often used for building serverless web APIs.
4. **Amazon SNS and SQS:** Lambda can process messages from SNS topics or SQS queues, making it ideal for building event-driven architectures.
5. **Amazon CloudWatch Events or EventBridge:** Schedules Lambda functions to run at regular intervals or in response to system events (e.g., every 10 minutes or daily tasks).
6. **Custom Event Sources:** Lambda can be triggered by external services using SDKs, enabling integration with non-AWS systems.

Each event source sends data to the Lambda function, which processes the input and executes the associated logic.

Lambda Limits and Quotas

When using AWS Lambda, there are certain **limits** to be aware of:

1. **Timeout:** Each Lambda function has a maximum execution time of **15 minutes**. If the function doesn't complete within this time, it is forcibly terminated.

2. **Memory Allocation:** You can allocate between **128 MB to 10 GB** of memory to a Lambda function. CPU power scales proportionally with the amount of memory allocated.

3. **Payload Size:**

- **Event Request Payload:** Maximum size of **6 MB** for synchronous invocations (e.g., HTTP requests) and **256 KB** for asynchronous invocations (e.g., S3 events).
- **Response Payload:** Maximum response size is **6 MB** for synchronous invocations.

1. **Concurrency:** By default, each AWS account is allowed **1,000 concurrent executions** per region. If more invocations are needed, you can request a quota increase.

2. **Deployment Package Size:**

- The **compressed deployment package** uploaded via the Lambda console or API has a limit of **50 MB**.
- The **uncompressed package** can be up to **250 MB**, including all libraries and dependencies.

1. **Environment Variables:** Lambda allows **4 KB** of environment variables to store configuration details such as API keys or connection strings.

2. **Execution Duration:** Functions that take longer than the allotted time will timeout. Plan for retry mechanisms or breaking down tasks into smaller units to avoid this.

Knowing these limits ensures your Lambda functions perform optimally and scale according to your needs.

Cold Starts and Warm Invocations

- **Cold Starts:**

- A cold start occurs when Lambda needs to spin up a new container to handle an incoming request. The container initialization includes loading the runtime environment, setting up the function, and executing initialization code. Cold starts cause a delay, typically ranging from a few hundred milliseconds to a few seconds, depending on several factors:
- **Runtime Language:** Heavier languages like Java or .NET generally have longer cold start times compared to lighter runtimes like Python or Node.js.
- **Package Size:** Larger deployment packages or functions with extensive initialization tasks can lead to slower cold starts.
- **Concurrency:** If your function experiences spikes in traffic, new containers must be created to handle additional requests, causing more cold starts.
- **Warm Invocations:**
- Warm invocations occur when Lambda reuses an already initialized container for subsequent requests. After the initial cold start, the same container can handle multiple invocations until AWS shuts it down after a period of inactivity (typically 5-15 minutes). Warm invocations are much faster, as there's no overhead from initialization.
- **Mitigating Cold Starts:**
- To minimize the performance impact of cold starts:
- **Provisioned Concurrency:** AWS offers **Provisioned Concurrency**, which keeps a predefined number of containers warm and ready to handle requests, significantly reducing cold start times.
- **Code Optimization:** Keep deployment packages small and reduce initialization tasks to optimize cold start performance.
- **Keep Functions Active:** Regularly invoke your function to prevent containers from being terminated (this can be achieved by setting up scheduled CloudWatch events).

Creating Lambda Functions in Python

Structure of a Lambda Function

AWS Lambda functions in Python follow a specific structure. Each function requires a **handler**, which is the entry point for AWS Lambda to execute the code. The handler receives two important parameters: event and context.

- **Event:** Contains data from the trigger (e.g., S3, API Gateway) that invoked the function.
- **Context:** Provides runtime information about the function invocation, such as memory limits, request ID, and log group details.

Here's a basic structure of a Lambda function in Python:

```python
Copy code
def lambda_handler(event, context):
    # Your function logic goes here
    response = {
        'statusCode': 200,
        'body': 'Hello from Lambda!'
    }
    return response
```

- **lambda_handler:** This is the entry point for the function. AWS Lambda looks for this handler when it runs the function.
- **Return Object:** The function returns a dictionary that contains the statusCode and body fields (this format is common for API Gateway responses).

Writing Basic Python Functions

To write a basic Lambda function in Python, you need to consider the event source. Here's an example of a simple Lambda function that returns a greeting based on input from the event.

```python
Copy code
def lambda_handler(event, context):
    name = event.get('name', 'Guest')  # Retrieve name from event,
    default to 'Guest'

    # Return a response
    response = {
        'statusCode': 200,
        'body': f'Hello, {name}!'
    }
    return response
```

Explanation:

- The event parameter in this example expects a key-value pair containing the key 'name'. If it's not present, the function defaults to greeting "Guest."
- The function returns an HTTP status code of 200 and a body containing the greeting.

This basic structure can be expanded to include more complex logic, such as interacting with other AWS services (e.g., S3, DynamoDB) or performing data processing tasks.

Testing Locally with AWS SAM and Docker

19

Testing Lambda functions locally before deployment is crucial to ensure they work correctly. AWS provides the **AWS Serverless Application Model (SAM)** and **Docker** to simulate Lambda's execution environment locally.

1. **Install AWS SAM CLI:**

- You can install AWS SAM CLI on your local machine:

```bash
Copy code
brew tap aws/tap
brew install aws-sam-cli
```

- For other platforms, follow the instructions on the official AWS SAM CLI installation page.

1. **Create a SAM Application:**

- You can initialize a new SAM application with a basic Lambda function by running:

```bash
Copy code
sam init
```

- Choose the runtime as Python and follow the prompts to set up the project structure.

1. **Writing Lambda Function with SAM:**

- After initializing the project, SAM creates a template.yaml file to define your Lambda function, API Gateway configurations, and other resources. The function code resides in a directory such as hello_world/app.py.

1. **Test Locally with Docker:**

- AWS SAM uses Docker to simulate the Lambda runtime environment. Run the following command to test the function locally:

```bash
Copy code
sam local invoke "HelloWorldFunction" --event event.json
```

- You can also run the function as an API by using:

```bash
Copy code
sam local start-api
```

- This will start a local server at http://127.0.0.1:3000 that you can use to test your Lambda function via HTTP requests.

Deploying Your First Lambda Function

After testing your Lambda function locally, you can deploy it to AWS Lambda. There are multiple ways to deploy a function, but we'll cover the simplest method using **AWS Management Console** and **AWS CLI**.

1. **Deploying via AWS Management Console:**

- Go to the AWS Lambda console and click **Create function**.
- Choose **Author from scratch**.
- Enter a name for your function (e.g., MyFirstPythonLambda) and select **Python** as the runtime.
- Create or assign an existing **IAM role** to the function, giving it the necessary permissions (e.g., access to S3 or CloudWatch).
- In the code editor, paste your function code. You can either write the function directly in the console or upload a .zip package containing your function and dependencies.
- Click **Deploy** to publish the function.
- You can manually invoke the function using the **Test** button or set up an event trigger (e.g., S3 or API Gateway).

1. **Deploying via AWS CLI:**

- First, ensure you have the **AWS CLI** configured on your local machine:

```bash
Copy code
aws configure
```

- Prepare a **deployment package** (a .zip file) that contains your Python function and any dependencies:

```bash
Copy code
zip my_function.zip lambda_function.py
```

- Deploy the function using the following AWS CLI command:

```bash
Copy code
aws lambda create-function \
  --function-name MyFirstPythonLambda \
  --runtime python3.8 \
  --role arn:aws:iam::123456789012:
role/lambda-execution-role \
  --handler lambda_function.lambda_handler \
  --zip-file fileb://my_function.zip
```

- Replace the **role ARN** with the appropriate role that grants Lambda execution permissions. This role should allow your function to log to CloudWatch and access any AWS resources it needs.

1. **Testing and Monitoring:**

- Once deployed, you can test the function by sending an event trigger (like an API call or an S3 upload) or by using the **Test** feature in the Lambda console.
- **CloudWatch Logs:** Each Lambda invocation is logged in CloudWatch. You can monitor your function's performance, check for errors, and log custom metrics.
- **Setting Up Triggers:** You can add triggers to your Lambda function (API Gateway, S3 events, DynamoDB, etc.) to invoke it automatically when certain conditions are met.

Managing Dependencies in AWS Lambda

When working with AWS Lambda functions in Python, it's common to use external libraries to add functionality or simplify tasks. Managing these dependencies properly is crucial to ensure that your Lambda functions run efficiently. Below are some key approaches and best practices for managing Python dependencies in AWS Lambda.

Handling Python Libraries in Lambda

AWS Lambda requires you to bundle any third-party Python libraries along with your Lambda function code because Lambda functions operate in isolated environments and do not have access to global or system-wide libraries.

Here's how you can handle Python libraries in Lambda:

1. **Include Libraries in Deployment Package:**

- For small dependencies or simple libraries, you can bundle them directly into your deployment package along with your Lambda function.
- Use pip to install the libraries locally in the directory where your function resides:

```bash
Copy code
pip install requests -t .
```

- This command installs the requests library in the current directory, making it part of your function's codebase. After that, create a .zip file that includes both your function and the installed libraries:

```bash
Copy code
zip -r my_function.zip .
```

1. **Deploy with Dependencies:**

- You can now upload the .zip file to AWS Lambda via the console or AWS CLI. Lambda will execute the function with the bundled dependencies.

This approach works for smaller dependencies, but if you're using large libraries or want to separate concerns, consider using Lambda Layers.

Using AWS Lambda Layers

Lambda Layers are a powerful feature that allows you to package libraries, dependencies, or even custom runtimes and share them across multiple Lambda functions. This reduces redundancy, simplifies deployment, and improves maintainability, especially when managing large libraries.

1. **Creating a Lambda Layer:**

- First, you'll need to package the Python libraries into a directory that matches Lambda's runtime environment. For Python, create a python/ directory and install the libraries there:

```bash
Copy code
mkdir -p python/lib/python3.8/site-packages
pip install requests -t
python/lib/python3.8/site-packages
```

- Once the libraries are installed, package the python/ directory into a .zip file:

```bash
Copy code
zip -r python_layer.zip python/
```

1. **Upload the Layer:**

- In the AWS Lambda console, navigate to the **Layers** section and click **Create Layer**.
- Upload the .zip file you created. You can also add a description and version number for the layer.

1. **Add the Layer to Your Lambda Function:**

- Once the layer is created, go to your Lambda function and add the layer by choosing **Layers** in the configuration section. Select the appropriate layer version.
- Now your Lambda function can access the libraries included in the layer without needing to package them with the function code.

1. **Reuse Across Functions:**

- The great advantage of Lambda Layers is that they can be reused across multiple Lambda functions, making it easier to maintain and update dependencies in a single place.

Packaging and Uploading Dependencies

For more complex or larger projects, packaging dependencies and uploading them requires careful management. Here are the steps for packaging and uploading dependencies efficiently:

1. **Using a Virtual Environment:**

- To isolate your dependencies, use Python's virtual environment tool:

```bash
Copy code
python3 -m venv myenv
source myenv/bin/activate
pip install requests
```

- Once the libraries are installed in the virtual environment, package the required dependencies into a .zip file:

```bash
Copy code
cd myenv/lib/python3.8/site-packages/
zip -r9 ../../../../my_function.zip .
```

1. **Add Your Code to the Zip File:**

- After packaging the dependencies, add your Lambda function code to the same .zip file:

```bash
bash
Copy code
cd ../../../../
zip -g my_function.zip lambda_function.py
```

1. **Upload to AWS:**

- You can then upload the .zip file via the AWS Management Console or AWS CLI:

```bash
bash
Copy code
aws lambda update-function-code \
  --function-name MyLambdaFunction \
  --zip-file fileb://my_function.zip
```

1. **Lambda with Large Dependencies:**

- If your deployment package exceeds the size limits (50 MB compressed, 250 MB uncompressed), consider offloading some of the libraries to Lambda Layers or using **Amazon S3** to host large deployment packages and linking them during function creation.

Best Practices for Managing Dependencies

Efficient management of dependencies can help ensure that your Lambda functions remain performant and easy to maintain. Here are some best practices:

1. **Use Lambda Layers for Shared Libraries:**

- If multiple Lambda functions use the same dependencies (e.g., common libraries such as boto3, requests), package them into a Lambda Layer to avoid duplicating them in each function's code package. This helps keep the function size smaller and simplifies updates.

1. **Minimize Deployment Package Size:**

- Keep the size of your deployment package small by only including the necessary libraries. Remove unnecessary files like documentation or test files that are part of the libraries.
- Use tools like pip —no-deps to install only the libraries you need without fetching unnecessary sub-dependencies:

```bash
Copy code
pip install requests --no-deps -t .
```

1. **Optimize for Cold Start Performance:**

- Large dependencies can slow down cold start times, particularly if Lambda needs to load a large package. Keep packages lean and avoid including libraries that aren't needed.
- Consider using **Provisioned Concurrency** for performance-critical functions, which keeps containers warm and reduces the effect of cold starts.

1. **Use Environment-Specific Layers:**

- If your application uses different libraries in development, testing, and production, create separate Lambda Layers for each environment. This allows for environment-specific optimizations and faster updates.

1. **Monitor and Update Dependencies Regularly:**

- Regularly update the libraries used in your Lambda functions to keep up with security patches and performance improvements. You can automate this process using CI/CD pipelines to build and test your Lambda packages with updated dependencies.

1. **Testing Dependencies Locally with AWS SAM:**

- Use AWS SAM to test Lambda functions with dependencies locally. This ensures that the function behaves as expected before deployment. SAM allows you to simulate Lambda's environment on your local machine.

By following these practices, you can ensure that your Lambda functions are scalable, maintainable, and performant when managing Python dependencies.

4o

You said:

Working with AWS Services in Lambda Integrating with Amazon S3 Interacting with DynamoDB Working with AWS API Gateway Using AWS Step Functions for Orchestration

ChatGPT said:

ChatGPT

Working with AWS Services in Lambda

AWS Lambda's integration with other AWS services is a powerful feature that enables serverless applications to interact with different components of the AWS ecosystem. Below, we'll explore how to integrate Lambda with **Amazon S3**, **DynamoDB**, **API Gateway**, and **Step Functions** to build robust, event-driven applications.

Integrating with Amazon S3

Amazon S3 (Simple Storage Service) is a popular object storage service, and Lambda can automatically respond to events in S3, such as file uploads, modifications, or deletions. Common use cases include file processing, image resizing, or log analysis.

1. **S3 Event Trigger for Lambda:**

- You can set up S3 to trigger Lambda when objects are added, modified, or deleted in an S3 bucket.
- For example, imagine uploading an image to S3 and having Lambda resize it.

1. **Setting Up an S3 Trigger:**

- **Step 1:** Go to the AWS Lambda Console, create a new Lambda function, and write your logic to handle S3 events.
- **Step 2:** Go to the S3 bucket where you want to enable the trigger.
- **Step 3:** In the **Properties** section of the bucket, add a **Trigger** under the **Event Notifications** section. Select your Lambda function as the destination and specify the event type (e.g., object created).

1. **Example Lambda Function (Processing S3 Object):** Here's an example of a Lambda function that processes an S3 event:

```python
Copy code
import boto3

def lambda_handler(event, context):
    s3 = boto3.client('s3')
    bucket_name = event['Records'][0]['s3']['bucket']['name']
    object_key = event['Records'][0]['s3']['object']['key']
```

```
# Retrieve the object from S3
s3_object = s3.get_object(Bucket=bucket_name, Key=object_key)
file_content = s3_object['Body'].read().decode('utf-8')

# Process the file (e.g., log its content or manipulate it)
print(f'Content of {object_key}: {file_content}')

return {
    'statusCode': 200,
    'body': 'File processed successfully'
}
```

1. **Best Practices for S3 Integration:**

- Use **S3 Object Lambda** to extend S3 operations if your processing logic needs to modify objects in S3.
- Optimize file processing by breaking down large files and processing them in chunks.
- Enable **S3 Transfer Acceleration** if you're working with large objects from different regions.

Interacting with DynamoDB

Amazon DynamoDB is a fully managed NoSQL database service that seamlessly integrates with Lambda. Lambda can be used to process real-time updates to DynamoDB tables, enabling serverless workflows for data processing.

1. **DynamoDB Streams as Event Sources:**

- You can enable **DynamoDB Streams** to capture changes to items in a DynamoDB table (e.g., inserts, updates, deletes) and trigger a Lambda function in response.
- Each change to a table can be passed to Lambda for processing, making it ideal for real-time analytics, data synchronization, or triggering

downstream workflows.

1. **Setting Up DynamoDB Stream Trigger:**

- **Step 1:** Go to your DynamoDB table and enable **Streams** in the settings.
- **Step 2:** In the Lambda console, create a new function and link it to the DynamoDB stream.
- **Step 3:** Configure the stream to capture the changes you're interested in (e.g., new items, updates).

1. **Example Lambda Function (DynamoDB Stream):** Here's an example that logs new records inserted into a DynamoDB table:

```python
Copy code
def lambda_handler(event, context):
    for record in event['Records']:
        if record['eventName'] == 'INSERT':
            new_record = record['dynamodb']['NewImage']
            print(f"New record added: {new_record}")

    return {
        'statusCode': 200,
        'body': 'DynamoDB event processed successfully'
    }
```

1. **Best Practices for DynamoDB Integration:**

- **Batch Processing:** Use **batch processing** to handle multiple DynamoDB stream records in a single Lambda invocation to reduce execution time and costs.
- **Error Handling:** Implement retry logic using **Dead Letter Queues (DLQ)** in case of failures during record processing.

- **Provisioned Concurrency:** If your DynamoDB streams are high-volume, you may want to use **Provisioned Concurrency** to minimize cold starts in Lambda.

Working with AWS API Gateway

Amazon API Gateway allows you to expose Lambda functions as HTTP(S) endpoints, which is useful for building RESTful APIs, backends for web or mobile apps, or handling incoming HTTP requests.

1. **Set Up an API Gateway Trigger:**

- **Step 1:** Create a Lambda function that will process HTTP requests. This function might handle GET, POST, PUT, or DELETE requests.
- **Step 2:** In the API Gateway console, create a new API.
- **Step 3:** Define resources (paths) and methods (GET, POST, etc.), and link each method to the Lambda function.

1. **Example Lambda Function (API Gateway):** Here's an example function that processes a request from API Gateway:

```python
Copy code
def lambda_handler(event, context):
    name = event['queryStringParameters']['name'] if 'name' in
    event['queryStringParameters'] else 'Guest'

    response = {
        'statusCode': 200,
        'body': f'Hello, {name}!'
    }
    return response
```

1. **Deploying the API:**

- After setting up the API and linking it to Lambda, deploy it to a **Stage** (e.g., Development, Production).
- You'll receive a public URL that can be used to invoke the Lambda function via HTTP requests.

1. **Best Practices for API Gateway Integration:**

- **Authorization:** Secure your API using **IAM roles**, **Cognito User Pools**, or **API Keys** for authentication and authorization.
- **Caching:** Enable caching in API Gateway to reduce the number of requests made to Lambda for frequently accessed data.
- **Throttling:** Set up **rate limiting** and **throttling** in API Gateway to protect your backend services from being overwhelmed by high traffic.

Using AWS Step Functions for Orchestration

AWS Step Functions is a service for orchestrating serverless workflows by chaining Lambda functions and other AWS services. This is useful for complex workflows, handling retries, or ensuring long-running tasks complete successfully.

1. **Creating a Step Functions State Machine:**

- **Step 1:** Define a **state machine** in Step Functions that consists of multiple states, each representing a step in your workflow.
- **Step 2:** Each step can invoke a Lambda function, pass data between steps, or handle error conditions like retries or fallback actions.
- **Step 3:** Write the state machine definition using **Amazon States Language** (JSON format).

1. **Example State Machine Definition (Basic Workflow):** The following is an example of a state machine definition that runs two Lambda functions in sequence:

```json
Copy code
{
  "Comment": "A simple Step Functions example",
  "StartAt": "Step1",
  "States": {
    "Step1": {
      "Type": "Task",
      "Resource":
      "arn:aws:lambda:REGION:ACCOUNT_ID:function:Function1",
      "Next": "Step2"
    },
    "Step2": {
      "Type": "Task",
      "Resource":
      "arn:aws:lambda:REGION:ACCOUNT_ID:function:Function2",
      "End": true
    }
  }
}
```

1. **Invoking the State Machine:**

- Once the state machine is created, you can invoke it via the AWS Management Console, API, or CLI. Each step executes the corresponding Lambda function in the workflow, passing data along the chain.

1. **Best Practices for Step Functions Integration:**

- **Error Handling:** Use Step Functions' built-in error handling and retry mechanisms to gracefully handle failures or timeouts in any step.
- **Long-Running Workflows:** Step Functions can manage long-running workflows by splitting tasks into smaller Lambda invocations or integrating with services like SQS.
- **Monitoring and Debugging:** Utilize the Step Functions console for

visualizing the execution flow and debugging failed steps.

By integrating AWS Lambda with services like Amazon S3, DynamoDB, API Gateway, and Step Functions, you can build scalable, event-driven applications without managing servers. Each of these integrations allows you to build automation, process real-time events, and create complex workflows efficiently.

Security Best Practices for Lambda Functions

E nsuring the security of AWS Lambda functions is critical, as these functions can interact with many AWS services, external APIs, and user data. Below are best practices for securing Lambda functions, covering **IAM roles and policies**, **permissions management**, **API Gateway security**, and **handling secrets**.

Understanding AWS IAM Roles and Policies

AWS Identity and Access Management (IAM) plays a key role in securing your Lambda functions by defining who or what can invoke your functions and what resources the functions themselves can access. IAM roles and policies control access at multiple layers:

1. **IAM Role for Lambda Function:**

- Every Lambda function operates with an **IAM execution role**, which determines the AWS resources it can access (e.g., S3, DynamoDB).
- This role should follow the **principle of least privilege**, meaning the role should only have the permissions needed to perform its specific tasks.

1. **IAM Policy for Invoking Lambda Functions:**

- You can create **resource-based policies** for Lambda functions that determine who or what services (e.g., API Gateway, SNS) are allowed to invoke them.
- This helps control which entities (users, roles, services) can trigger the function and ensures that unauthorized access is blocked.

Example IAM Role Policy:

```json
Copy code
{
    "Version": "2012-10-17",
    "Statement": [
        {
            "Effect": "Allow",
            "Action": "dynamodb:*",
            "Resource": "arn:aws:dynamodb:
us-east-1:123456789012:table/my-table"
        },
        {
            "Effect": "Deny",
            "Action": "s3:DeleteObject",
            "Resource": "arn:aws:s3:::my-bucket/*"
        }
    ]
}
```

This policy allows the Lambda function to access DynamoDB but denies any attempt to delete objects from an S3 bucket.

Managing Permissions for Lambda Functions

Properly managing permissions ensures that Lambda functions only have access to the resources they need. This can be achieved using the following best practices:

1. **Grant the Minimum Required Permissions:**

- Assign the **least privilege** to Lambda functions by allowing only the actions and resources they need to operate. For example, if a function only needs to read from an S3 bucket, limit permissions to s3:GetObject.

- Use IAM roles for Lambda functions that are specific to their purpose instead of using broad roles.

1. **Control Permissions with Resource-Based Policies:**

- In addition to using IAM roles, Lambda functions can have **resource-based policies** that control which AWS services or accounts can invoke the function.
- This allows you to restrict access to Lambda functions from certain services (like API Gateway or S3) and ensures tighter control over who can trigger the function.

1. **Monitor Lambda Access Using CloudTrail:**

- **AWS CloudTrail** can log and monitor who invokes Lambda functions and what resources the function interacts with. This provides a history of activity and helps identify potential security issues.

1. **Avoid Over-Privileged IAM Roles:**

- Avoid assigning overly broad roles like AdministratorAccess to Lambda functions. Instead, use tailored policies that allow access only to necessary resources and actions.

Securing API Gateway Endpoints

If you're exposing Lambda functions through **Amazon API Gateway**, it's important to secure these endpoints to prevent unauthorized access and misuse.

1. **Enable Authentication and Authorization:**

- Use **AWS IAM roles, Amazon Cognito User Pools**, or **Lambda authorizers** to control access to your API Gateway endpoints.
- **Cognito User Pools:** Allow users to authenticate through popular identity providers (e.g., Google, Facebook) or using your custom user directory.
- **Lambda Authorizers:** You can create custom authorization logic by using Lambda functions to validate requests before they reach the main function.
- **IAM Authorization:** API Gateway can be secured using IAM policies to restrict who can call the API.

1. **Use HTTPS for Secure Communication:**

- Ensure that all communication between clients and API Gateway is encrypted using HTTPS. API Gateway automatically provides an SSL endpoint (https://), and you should enforce this in your application.
- Optionally, enable **AWS WAF (Web Application Firewall)** to protect API endpoints from common web attacks, like SQL injection or cross-site scripting.

1. **Enable Throttling and Rate Limiting:**

- Set **rate limits** in API Gateway to control the number of requests that can hit your Lambda functions over a period of time. This prevents abuse from a single user or application and helps avoid overloading your backend.
- Define **usage plans** with throttling and quota limits for different API consumers.

1. **Protect Against DDoS Attacks:**

- API Gateway is integrated with **AWS Shield**, a managed Distributed Denial of Service (DDoS) protection service. Ensure it's enabled to protect your APIs from volumetric attacks.

Handling Secrets and Sensitive Data with AWS Secrets Manager

Many Lambda functions need to access sensitive data like API keys, database credentials, or other secrets. Storing these securely is essential to avoid leaks and unauthorized access.

1. **Use AWS Secrets Manager:**

- **AWS Secrets Manager** allows you to securely store, manage, and retrieve sensitive information such as database credentials, API keys, or OAuth tokens. The service encrypts secrets with AWS KMS (Key Management Service).
- Lambda functions can securely retrieve secrets from Secrets Manager during execution, avoiding the need to hard-code sensitive information.

1. **Encrypt Environment Variables:**

- If you use environment variables to store configuration data, ensure that sensitive information (e.g., access tokens) is encrypted using **AWS Key Management Service (KMS)**.
- When configuring a Lambda function, enable encryption for specific environment variables by using a KMS key.

Example (Retrieving Secrets from Secrets Manager):

```python
Copy code
import boto3
import os

def lambda_handler(event, context):
    secret_name = os.getenv('SECRET_NAME')
    region_name = os.getenv('AWS_REGION')
```

```python
    # Create a Secrets Manager client
    client = boto3.client('secretsmanager',
region_name=region_name)

    # Retrieve the secret
    get_secret_value_response =
    client.get_secret_value(SecretId=secret_name)
    secret = get_secret_value_response['SecretString']

    # Use the secret for your function's logic
    print(f"The secret value is: {secret}")

    return {
        'statusCode': 200,
        'body': 'Secret retrieved successfully!'
    }
```

This example shows how a Lambda function retrieves a secret from AWS Secrets Manager securely.

1. **Rotate Secrets Regularly:**

- AWS Secrets Manager can automatically rotate secrets for supported databases and services. Set up automatic rotation to ensure that sensitive credentials are updated periodically without manual intervention.

1. **Audit Secret Access:**

- Use **CloudTrail** and **AWS Config** to monitor and audit access to your secrets. Ensure that access to secrets is logged and reviewed regularly to detect any unauthorized access.

Additional Best Practices:

1. **Encrypt Data at Rest and In-Transit:**

- Always encrypt sensitive data, whether it's stored in databases (data at rest) or passed between services (data in-transit). Use **AWS KMS** to manage encryption keys.

1. **Audit and Monitor Lambda Security:**

- Use **AWS CloudWatch** to monitor Lambda function activity and **AWS Config** to audit configurations. Enable **CloudTrail** logs for comprehensive monitoring and auditing of who accesses your Lambda functions and what actions are taken.

1. **Enable Multi-Factor Authentication (MFA):**

- For users and services interacting with Lambda, enable **MFA** to provide an additional layer of security during authentication.

Security Best Practices for Lambda Functions

E nsuring the security of AWS Lambda functions is critical, as these functions can interact with many AWS services, external APIs, and user data. Below are best practices for securing Lambda functions, covering **IAM roles and policies, permissions management, API Gateway security**, and **handling secrets**.

Understanding AWS IAM Roles and Policies

AWS Identity and Access Management (IAM) plays a key role in securing your Lambda functions by defining who or what can invoke your functions and what resources the functions themselves can access. IAM roles and policies control access at multiple layers:

1. **IAM Role for Lambda Function:**

- Every Lambda function operates with an **IAM execution role**, which determines the AWS resources it can access (e.g., S3, DynamoDB).
- This role should follow the **principle of least privilege**, meaning the role should only have the permissions needed to perform its specific tasks.

1. **IAM Policy for Invoking Lambda Functions:**

- You can create **resource-based policies** for Lambda functions that determine who or what services (e.g., API Gateway, SNS) are allowed to invoke them.
- This helps control which entities (users, roles, services) can trigger the function and ensures that unauthorized access is blocked.

Example IAM Role Policy:

```json
Copy code
{
  "Version": "2012-10-17",
  "Statement": [
    {
      "Effect": "Allow",
      "Action": "dynamodb:*",
      "Resource": "arn:aws:dynamodb:
us-east-1:123456789012:table/my-table"
    },
    {
      "Effect": "Deny",
      "Action": "s3:DeleteObject",
      "Resource": "arn:aws:s3:::my-bucket/*"
    }
  ]
}
```

This policy allows the Lambda function to access DynamoDB but denies any attempt to delete objects from an S3 bucket.

Managing Permissions for Lambda Functions

Properly managing permissions ensures that Lambda functions only have access to the resources they need. This can be achieved using the following best practices:

1. **Grant the Minimum Required Permissions:**

- Assign the **least privilege** to Lambda functions by allowing only the actions and resources they need to operate. For example, if a function only needs to read from an S3 bucket, limit permissions to s3:GetObject.

- Use IAM roles for Lambda functions that are specific to their purpose instead of using broad roles.

1. **Control Permissions with Resource-Based Policies:**

- In addition to using IAM roles, Lambda functions can have **resource-based policies** that control which AWS services or accounts can invoke the function.
- This allows you to restrict access to Lambda functions from certain services (like API Gateway or S3) and ensures tighter control over who can trigger the function.

1. **Monitor Lambda Access Using CloudTrail:**

- **AWS CloudTrail** can log and monitor who invokes Lambda functions and what resources the function interacts with. This provides a history of activity and helps identify potential security issues.

1. **Avoid Over-Privileged IAM Roles:**

- Avoid assigning overly broad roles like AdministratorAccess to Lambda functions. Instead, use tailored policies that allow access only to necessary resources and actions.

Securing API Gateway Endpoints

If you're exposing Lambda functions through **Amazon API Gateway**, it's important to secure these endpoints to prevent unauthorized access and misuse.

1. **Enable Authentication and Authorization:**

- Use **AWS IAM roles, Amazon Cognito User Pools,** or **Lambda authorizers** to control access to your API Gateway endpoints.
- **Cognito User Pools:** Allow users to authenticate through popular identity providers (e.g., Google, Facebook) or using your custom user directory.
- **Lambda Authorizers:** You can create custom authorization logic by using Lambda functions to validate requests before they reach the main function.
- **IAM Authorization:** API Gateway can be secured using IAM policies to restrict who can call the API.

1. **Use HTTPS for Secure Communication:**

- Ensure that all communication between clients and API Gateway is encrypted using HTTPS. API Gateway automatically provides an SSL endpoint (https://), and you should enforce this in your application.
- Optionally, enable **AWS WAF (Web Application Firewall)** to protect API endpoints from common web attacks, like SQL injection or cross-site scripting.

1. **Enable Throttling and Rate Limiting:**

- Set **rate limits** in API Gateway to control the number of requests that can hit your Lambda functions over a period of time. This prevents abuse from a single user or application and helps avoid overloading your backend.
- Define **usage plans** with throttling and quota limits for different API consumers.

1. **Protect Against DDoS Attacks:**

- API Gateway is integrated with **AWS Shield,** a managed Distributed Denial of Service (DDoS) protection service. Ensure it's enabled to protect your APIs from volumetric attacks.

Handling Secrets and Sensitive Data with AWS Secrets Manager

Many Lambda functions need to access sensitive data like API keys, database credentials, or other secrets. Storing these securely is essential to avoid leaks and unauthorized access.

1. **Use AWS Secrets Manager:**

- **AWS Secrets Manager** allows you to securely store, manage, and retrieve sensitive information such as database credentials, API keys, or OAuth tokens. The service encrypts secrets with AWS KMS (Key Management Service).
- Lambda functions can securely retrieve secrets from Secrets Manager during execution, avoiding the need to hard-code sensitive information.

1. **Encrypt Environment Variables:**

- If you use environment variables to store configuration data, ensure that sensitive information (e.g., access tokens) is encrypted using **AWS Key Management Service (KMS)**.
- When configuring a Lambda function, enable encryption for specific environment variables by using a KMS key.

Example (Retrieving Secrets from Secrets Manager):

```python
Copy code
import boto3
import os

def lambda_handler(event, context):
    secret_name = os.getenv('SECRET_NAME')
    region_name = os.getenv('AWS_REGION')
```

```
    # Create a Secrets Manager client
    client = boto3.client('secretsmanager',
region_name=region_name)

    # Retrieve the secret
    get_secret_value_response =
    client.get_secret_value(SecretId=secret_name)
    secret = get_secret_value_response['SecretString']

    # Use the secret for your function's logic
    print(f"The secret value is: {secret}")

    return {
        'statusCode': 200,
        'body': 'Secret retrieved successfully!'
    }
```

This example shows how a Lambda function retrieves a secret from AWS Secrets Manager securely.

1. **Rotate Secrets Regularly:**

• AWS Secrets Manager can automatically rotate secrets for supported databases and services. Set up automatic rotation to ensure that sensitive credentials are updated periodically without manual intervention.

1. **Audit Secret Access:**

• Use **CloudTrail** and **AWS Config** to monitor and audit access to your secrets. Ensure that access to secrets is logged and reviewed regularly to detect any unauthorized access.

Additional Best Practices:

1. **Encrypt Data at Rest and In-Transit:**

- Always encrypt sensitive data, whether it's stored in databases (data at rest) or passed between services (data in-transit). Use **AWS KMS** to manage encryption keys.

1. **Audit and Monitor Lambda Security:**

- Use **AWS CloudWatch** to monitor Lambda function activity and **AWS Config** to audit configurations. Enable **CloudTrail** logs for comprehensive monitoring and auditing of who accesses your Lambda functions and what actions are taken.

1. **Enable Multi-Factor Authentication (MFA):**

- For users and services interacting with Lambda, enable **MFA** to provide an additional layer of security during authentication.

Optimizing Python Code for AWS Lambda

AWS Lambda's performance depends heavily on how efficiently the code and resources are managed. Optimizing for factors such as cold start latency, timeouts, resource usage, and debugging can significantly improve the performance and cost-effectiveness of your Lambda functions. Below are strategies to optimize Python code for Lambda.

Reducing Cold Start Latency

Cold starts occur when AWS Lambda initializes a new execution environment (container) to process an event. Cold start times can be more noticeable in Python functions with larger packages or when functions are invoked infrequently.

1. **Use Lightweight Dependencies:**

- **Minimize the size of your deployment package** by including only essential libraries. The larger the package, the longer the cold start time due to the need to download and initialize libraries.
- Remove unnecessary dependencies or switch to lightweight alternatives when possible (e.g., use requests for HTTP instead of boto3 if you don't need AWS-specific features).

1. **Optimize Code Initialization:**

- Keep initialization code (e.g., database connections, configuration loading) outside the handler function but minimize its complexity. Placing heavy initialization logic inside the handler can delay execution.
- Use environment variables or AWS Secrets Manager to pass configurations efficiently, reducing the overhead of reading files during the cold start.

1. **Provisioned Concurrency:**

- Use **Provisioned Concurrency** to keep containers "warm" and pre-initialized, significantly reducing cold start times. This is ideal for latency-sensitive applications or those that require consistent performance.

1. **Steps to enable Provisioned Concurrency:**

- In the AWS Lambda console, navigate to your function.
- Under **Concurrency**, choose **Provisioned Concurrency** and specify the number of pre-warmed containers.
- AWS will ensure that a fixed number of function instances are always ready to serve incoming requests.

1. **Use the Right Python Runtime Version:**

- Newer Python runtimes (e.g., Python 3.8+) are often optimized for performance and may experience reduced cold start times compared to older versions.

Managing Timeouts and Retries

AWS Lambda functions have a **maximum execution timeout** of 15 minutes, and controlling timeouts and retries helps ensure efficient function execution and reduces unnecessary costs.

1. **Set Appropriate Timeouts:**

- Always configure the **timeout** based on the expected execution time of your function. By default, Lambda functions have a 3-second timeout, but this may need to be adjusted depending on the use case.
- Avoid unnecessarily long timeouts. If a function usually completes in 2 seconds, a 15-minute timeout could cause unnecessary waiting in case of failure.

1. Example:

```bash
Copy code
aws lambda update-function-configuration \
  --function-name MyFunction \
  --timeout 10  # Timeout set to 10 seconds
```

1. **Handle Retries Gracefully:**

- AWS Lambda automatically retries asynchronous invocations in case of failure. You should design your code to handle retries gracefully by making operations **idempotent** (i.e., ensure repeated executions produce the same outcome).
- For asynchronous invocations, retries happen twice by default (with delays), which can be configured. If failures persist, use **dead-letter queues (DLQ)** to capture the failed events and process them later.

1. **Exponential Backoff for Retries:**

- When working with external APIs or services, use **exponential backoff** in your code to handle transient errors or rate limits effectively. This reduces the risk of overloading third-party services.

1. Example (Exponential Backoff):

```python
Copy code
import time

def exponential_backoff(attempt):
    time.sleep(2 ** attempt)

def lambda_handler(event, context):
    for attempt in range(5):
        try:
            # Attempt an operation (e.g., API request)
            response = my_external_service_request()
            return response
        except Exception as e:
            exponential_backoff(attempt)
```

Efficient Resource Usage (Memory and CPU)

AWS Lambda charges based on the amount of memory allocated and the duration of execution. Optimizing the memory and CPU allocation can help balance cost and performance.

1. **Memory Allocation and CPU Power:**

- Lambda functions are assigned CPU resources proportional to the allocated memory. Increasing memory not only provides more RAM but also allocates more CPU power.
- If your function is CPU-bound (e.g., heavy computation tasks), increasing the memory can lead to faster execution times, reducing overall cost by completing tasks quicker.

1. **Tuning Memory Example:**

- Use the AWS CLI to adjust memory allocation:

```bash
bash
Copy code
aws lambda update-function-configuration \
  --function-name MyFunction \
  --memory-size 1024  # 1GB of memory
```

- Test your function with different memory settings and analyze the cost-performance trade-off using **AWS CloudWatch** metrics.

1. **Avoid Over-Allocation:**

- Avoid assigning more memory than necessary. If your function uses minimal CPU and memory, keeping memory allocation low (e.g., 128 MB) can save costs.
- For data processing tasks that involve handling smaller payloads, you can start with lower memory settings and scale up based on performance requirements.

1. **Leverage External Services for Long-Running Tasks:**

- Offload long-running tasks, such as video transcoding or large file processing, to services like **AWS Step Functions**, **AWS Batch**, or **Amazon SQS**, which are more suitable for complex workflows and allow Lambda to focus on quick, event-driven tasks.

Profiling and Debugging Lambda Functions

Understanding the performance of your Lambda functions and identifying bottlenecks are essential for optimization. AWS provides several tools for profiling and debugging.

1. **CloudWatch Logs and Metrics:**

- **AWS CloudWatch** logs and metrics are automatically available for all Lambda functions. These logs provide key insights into function invocations, errors, and latency.
- **Memory Usage:** Monitor memory usage metrics in CloudWatch to ensure your function is using its allocated resources efficiently. If memory utilization is consistently low, you may want to reduce the memory allocation to save costs.

1. **AWS X-Ray for Tracing:**

- **AWS X-Ray** is a tracing service that helps identify performance bottlenecks by providing detailed insights into how your Lambda function interacts with other AWS services (e.g., S3, DynamoDB, API Gateway).
- By enabling X-Ray for your Lambda function, you can trace each request, measure latency, and detect slow components in your function's execution.

1. **Steps to Enable X-Ray:**

- Go to the Lambda console, select your function, and in the **Monitoring and Operations Tools** section, enable **Active Tracing**.
- Use X-Ray's visual interface to view the execution path of requests and drill down into specific segments to identify latency issues or errors.

1. **AWS Lambda Power Tuning Tool:**

- AWS provides a **Lambda Power Tuning** tool that helps you optimize resource allocation by testing your function at different memory settings and suggesting the most cost-effective configuration.
- The tool runs multiple tests and provides a visualization of cost vs. execution time, allowing you to choose the optimal setting for your function.

1. **Tool Setup:**

- Install the tool via the AWS Serverless Application Repository, and use it to test different memory settings.

1. **Third-Party Profiling Tools:**

- You can also use third-party monitoring and profiling tools (e.g., **Datadog, Lumigo, New Relic**) that offer detailed insights into Lambda function performance, including memory usage, CPU bottlenecks, and invocation patterns.

Logging and Monitoring AWS Lambda Functions

E ffective logging and monitoring are critical for ensuring the stability, performance, and security of your AWS Lambda functions. AWS provides tools like **CloudWatch, X-Ray**, and **CloudWatch Alarms** to give detailed insights into your Lambda functions' behavior and performance. Below is a guide to logging and monitoring Lambda functions using these tools.

Using AWS CloudWatch for Logs

Amazon CloudWatch Logs automatically collects and stores logs generated by AWS Lambda. Every Lambda function has access to CloudWatch, and logs from each function invocation are stored in CloudWatch for review and analysis.

1. **Enabling CloudWatch Logging for Lambda:**

- By default, Lambda automatically sends function logs to CloudWatch. No extra setup is required as long as your Lambda function's **execution role** has the necessary permissions (logs:CreateLogGroup, logs:CreateLogStream, logs:PutLogEvents).
- Each Lambda function generates its own **log group** in CloudWatch with the format /aws/lambda/<function-name>.

1. **Viewing Logs in CloudWatch:**

- Navigate to the **CloudWatch Console**.
- Select **Log Groups,** then choose your Lambda function's log group to view log streams for each invocation.
- Each log stream provides detailed information such as start and end times, memory usage, errors, and any log statements you include in your code.

1. **Adding Custom Log Statements:**

- You can add custom logging using Python's logging module or simple print() statements.
- Example:

```python
Copy code
import logging

logger = logging.getLogger()
logger.setLevel(logging.INFO)

def lambda_handler(event, context):
    logger.info('This is an info message')
    logger.error('This is an error message')
    print('This will also be logged in CloudWatch')
```

1. **Retention Policy:**

- By default, CloudWatch Logs retain logs indefinitely. You can configure **retention periods** (e.g., 1 day, 1 week, etc.) to automatically delete old logs and reduce costs.
- Set a retention policy in the **CloudWatch Console** under the log group's

settings.

Setting Up Custom Metrics with CloudWatch

Custom metrics allow you to track specific performance data that is not captured by default CloudWatch metrics. You can create custom metrics to monitor application-specific details like request counts, processing times, or error rates.

1. **Publishing Custom Metrics:**

- Use the put_metric_data() function from **boto3** to publish custom metrics from within your Lambda function.

1. Example:

```python
Copy code
import boto3
import time

cloudwatch = boto3.client('cloudwatch')

def lambda_handler(event, context):
    start_time = time.time()

    # Simulate processing
    processing_time = time.time() - start_time

    # Publish a custom metric for processing time
    cloudwatch.put_metric_data(
        Namespace='MyApp',
        MetricData=[
            {
                'MetricName': 'ProcessingTime',
                'Dimensions': [
```

```
            {
                'Name': 'FunctionName',
                'Value': context.function_name
            },
        ],
        'Unit': 'Seconds',
        'Value': processing_time
    },
  ]
)
```

- **Namespace:** Group your custom metrics under a specific namespace (e.g., MyApp) to distinguish them from AWS default metrics.
- **Dimensions:** You can specify custom dimensions, such as function name or region, to categorize metrics.

1. **Viewing Custom Metrics in CloudWatch:**

- Navigate to the **CloudWatch Console** and select **Metrics**.
- Choose the **Custom Namespaces** category to view metrics under your custom namespace (e.g., MyApp).
- From here, you can create dashboards or set up alarms based on these custom metrics.

Debugging with AWS X-Ray

AWS X-Ray is a distributed tracing service that helps you analyze and debug the execution of your Lambda functions and their interactions with other AWS services (e.g., S3, DynamoDB, API Gateway). It provides insights into the execution flow and identifies performance bottlenecks or errors.

1. **Enabling AWS X-Ray Tracing:**

- In the **Lambda Console**, navigate to your Lambda function.

- Under **Monitoring and Operations Tools**, enable **Active Tracing** to allow Lambda to send trace data to X-Ray.
- Ensure the Lambda execution role has permissions to write to X-Ray (xray:PutTraceSegments and xray:PutTelemetryRecords).

1. **Using X-Ray SDK in Lambda:**

- To get more detailed traces, you can use the **AWS X-Ray SDK** in your Python Lambda function. Install the SDK by including the aws-xray-sdk in your deployment package.

1. Example:

```python
Copy code
from aws_xray_sdk.core import xray_recorder
from aws_xray_sdk.core import patch_all

patch_all()  # Automatically trace supported
libraries like boto3, requests

def lambda_handler(event, context):
    xray_recorder.begin_segment('LambdaFunctionSegment')

    # Add custom annotations or metadata
    xray_recorder.put_annotation('User', event.get('user',
    'Unknown'))

    # Simulate a process
    result = process_event(event)

    xray_recorder.end_segment()
    return result
```

1. **Viewing X-Ray Traces:**

- Navigate to the **X-Ray Console**, where you'll see a visual trace of the function execution.
- X-Ray provides a **service map** showing interactions between Lambda and other AWS services, along with detailed information on request latency, error rates, and any failed services.
- Use the **timeline** view to see how long each component took to execute and identify performance bottlenecks.

1. **Performance Insights with X-Ray:**

- X-Ray highlights problematic areas such as slow API responses, high retries, or cold starts.
- You can add **annotations** and **metadata** to your traces, allowing you to filter and analyze specific aspects of your Lambda execution.

Creating Alerts for Lambda Performance

Monitoring Lambda functions is useful, but creating alerts ensures that you're immediately notified when something goes wrong. **CloudWatch Alarms** can be set up to trigger notifications based on metrics such as invocation errors, duration, or custom metrics.

1. **Setting Up a CloudWatch Alarm:**

- Navigate to the **CloudWatch Console** and select **Alarms** from the sidebar.
- Click **Create Alarm** and select the Lambda function's metric you want to monitor (e.g., **Errors, Throttles, Duration**).
- Define the conditions for the alarm. For example, trigger an alarm if the **Errors** exceed 5 in a 5-minute period.

1. **Sending Notifications with SNS:**

- Configure the alarm to send notifications through **Amazon SNS (Simple**

Notification Service).

- Create an SNS topic if you don't already have one, and subscribe your email or SMS to receive alerts.
- When the alarm state changes (e.g., the error count exceeds the threshold), an email or SMS notification is sent to alert you.

1. **Example: Setting up an Error Rate Alarm:**

- Select the **Errors** metric for your Lambda function.
- Set the condition: **Error count greater than 1** for a period of **5 minutes**.
- Link the alarm to an SNS topic to send alerts.

1. **Automated Remediation:**

- Combine CloudWatch Alarms with **AWS Lambda** to perform automated remediation. For example, if an alarm detects a high error rate, trigger another Lambda function to scale resources or restart services.

1. **Creating Dashboards:**

- Use **CloudWatch Dashboards** to visualize key Lambda metrics in one place. Create custom dashboards that display invocation count, error rates, memory usage, and duration across multiple functions.
- Dashboards help you keep an eye on real-time Lambda performance and quickly identify trends or issues.

Advanced Python Features in Lambda

AWS Lambda offers advanced capabilities to optimize your Python functions for various use cases, including handling concurrency, managing asynchronous invocations, customizing runtimes, and managing multiple environments. Below, we cover these advanced Python features and how to utilize them effectively.

Handling Concurrency and Scaling

AWS Lambda automatically scales to handle requests, invoking as many instances of your function as needed based on the incoming workload. This elasticity is one of the key advantages of serverless computing. Understanding how concurrency and scaling work in Lambda is critical to optimizing performance and cost.

1. **Concurrent Execution:**

- **Concurrency** refers to the number of function instances running simultaneously in response to incoming events.
- Each Lambda function can handle a single event per execution. If multiple events are received, Lambda scales by running multiple instances of the function concurrently.
- AWS Lambda has a soft limit of **1,000 concurrent executions** per region, but this can be increased by submitting a request to AWS.

1. Provisioned Concurrency:

- By default, Lambda handles **on-demand scaling**. However, **Provisioned Concurrency** can be used to reduce cold start latency and ensure that a set number of function instances are pre-warmed and ready to handle requests instantly.
- Provisioned concurrency is especially useful for latency-sensitive applications like real-time APIs or user-facing services.

1. Example: Enabling Provisioned Concurrency

```bash
Copy code
aws lambda put-provisioned-concurrency-config \
  --function-name MyLambdaFunction \
  --qualifier $LATEST \
  --provisioned-concurrent-executions 10
```

1. Throttling and Burst Concurrency:

- AWS Lambda throttles requests that exceed the account's concurrent execution limit. Throttled requests are automatically retried for asynchronous invocations but return an error for synchronous invocations (like API Gateway).
- Lambda allows **burst concurrency** in short periods of high load, with AWS managing additional requests for a short time.

1. Best Practices for Handling Concurrency:

- **Idempotency:** Ensure that your Lambda function is **idempotent**, meaning repeated invocations of the same event should not lead to inconsistent or erroneous results.

- **Concurrency Limits:** Set **reserved concurrency** limits to avoid overloading dependent services. For example, limit the number of concurrent Lambda executions to prevent overwhelming a downstream DynamoDB table.

Using Asynchronous Invocations

In some cases, you may want to invoke a Lambda function asynchronously. This allows your function to return immediately without waiting for the function to complete, useful for tasks like background processing, log ingestion, or event-based architectures.

1. **Asynchronous Invocation Model:**

- When you invoke a Lambda function asynchronously, AWS automatically queues the event and processes it in the background. This allows your main application to continue without waiting for Lambda's response.
- AWS Lambda attempts to process the event twice by default in case of a failure, with exponential backoff between retries.

1. **Example: Asynchronous Invocation Using AWS CLI**

```bash
Copy code
aws lambda invoke \
  --function-name MyLambdaFunction \
  --invocation-type Event \
  outputfile.txt
```

1. **Dead Letter Queues (DLQs):**

- If Lambda cannot successfully process an event after retries, you can configure a **Dead Letter Queue (DLQ)**, such as an SQS queue or an SNS topic, to capture failed events. This ensures that no data is lost, and failed events can be analyzed or retried later.

1. **Configuring a Dead Letter Queue:**

- In the Lambda console, under **Asynchronous invocation**, specify an SQS or SNS resource as the DLQ for your function.

1. **Event Source Mapping for Asynchronous Processing:**

- For services like DynamoDB or Kinesis, you can create **event source mappings** to trigger Lambda functions asynchronously when changes occur. This is common in event-driven architectures where data changes trigger automated processing.

Custom Runtimes for Advanced Use Cases

AWS Lambda supports a wide range of runtimes (Python, Node.js, Java, etc.), but sometimes you may need a custom runtime for a specialized use case, such as using a non-supported language or custom libraries.

1. **Using AWS Lambda Layers for Custom Runtimes:**

- **Lambda Layers** allow you to package external libraries, dependencies, or even entire runtimes to share across multiple Lambda functions. This is useful if you need a specific version of Python or a language not natively supported by AWS Lambda.

1. **Steps to Create a Custom Runtime Using Layers:**

- **Step 1:** Package your runtime as a Layer. This could include custom binaries or libraries required for your application.
- **Step 2:** Upload the runtime Layer to Lambda and associate it with your function.

- **Step 3:** AWS Lambda will load your custom runtime when the function is invoked.

1. **Example: Using a Custom Python Runtime Layer**

- Create a bootstrap file for the custom runtime, then upload the layer:

```bash
Copy code
mkdir my-python-runtime
echo '#!/bin/sh' > my-python-runtime/bootstrap
chmod 755 my-python-runtime/bootstrap
zip -r my-python-runtime.zip my-python-runtime/
aws lambda publish-layer-version
--layer-name CustomPythonRuntime
--zip-file fileb://my-python-runtime.zip
```

1. **Custom Runtimes for Unsupported Languages:**

- If you need to run Lambda functions in a language not supported by AWS (e.g., Rust, Go, or PHP), you can build a custom runtime using Lambda Layers.

1. **Best Practices for Custom Runtimes:**

- Ensure that the custom runtime is as lightweight as possible to reduce cold start latency.
- Test the custom runtime thoroughly before deploying it to production to avoid runtime errors.

Managing Multiple Environments (Dev, Test, Prod)

In most applications, you will need separate environments (e.g., **development**, **testing**, and **production**) to ensure smooth deployment and minimize risk. Lambda makes it easy to manage multiple environments.

1. **Environment Variables:**

- Use **environment variables** to differentiate between environments without changing code. You can set environment-specific values like database connection strings, API keys, or logging levels directly in the Lambda configuration.

1. **Example: Setting Environment Variables**

```bash
Copy code
aws lambda update-function-configuration \
  --function-name MyFunction \
  --environment Variables="{ENV='prod',
  DB_HOST='prod-db.example.com'}"
```

1. **Lambda Aliases and Versions:**

- Use **Lambda Versions** and **Aliases** to manage deployments across different environments. Each published version of your Lambda function is immutable and can be referenced using an alias (e.g., dev, test, prod).
- This approach allows you to promote a specific version to production while keeping other versions for testing or development.

1. **Example: Create and Use Aliases**

- Publish a new version:

```bash
bash
Copy code
aws lambda publish-version --function-name MyFunction
```

- Create an alias for this version:

```bash
bash
Copy code
aws lambda create-alias \
  --function-name MyFunction \
  --name prod \
  --function-version 2
```

1. **Infrastructure as Code (IaC):**

- Use tools like **AWS CloudFormation** or **AWS SAM** (Serverless Application Model) to define your Lambda infrastructure as code. This ensures consistent deployment across multiple environments.
- You can create templates that specify environment-specific resources like databases, queues, or API gateways for each environment.

1. **CI/CD Pipelines for Lambda:**

- Implement **CI/CD pipelines** using tools like **AWS CodePipeline** or third-party services like **GitLab** or **Jenkins** to automate deployment to different environments.
- Set up automated tests in development and staging environments before promoting code to production.

1. **Best Practices for Environment Management:**

- Keep separate Lambda functions or aliases for different environments (e.g., MyFunction-dev, MyFunction-prod).
- Secure environment-specific credentials using **AWS Secrets Manager** or **AWS Parameter Store** to ensure production keys are never exposed in development environments.

Handling Errors and Retries in Lambda Functions

H andling errors and retries effectively in AWS Lambda functions is essential for building resilient, fault-tolerant serverless applications. Lambda provides several mechanisms for error handling, including automatic retries, Dead Letter Queues (DLQs), and Lambda Destinations. Below, we'll explore common error types, how to handle them, and best practices for building fault-tolerant applications.

Common Error Types and How to Handle Them

When Lambda functions encounter errors, they fall into two broad categories: **handled exceptions** and **unhandled exceptions**.

1. **Handled Exceptions:**

- Handled exceptions occur when you anticipate an error and explicitly handle it in your code using try-except blocks in Python.
- These are typically recoverable errors, such as timeouts when making API requests, temporary resource unavailability, or invalid input.

1. **Example: Handling a Timeout Error**

```python
Copy code
import requests
from requests.exceptions import Timeout

def lambda_handler(event, context):
    try:
        response = requests.get
('https://example.com', timeout=5)
        return response.content
    except Timeout:
        return {
            'statusCode': 504,
            'body': 'Request timed out, please try again later.'
        }
```

1. **Unhandled Exceptions:**

- Unhandled exceptions occur when the function fails to catch an error, causing the Lambda function to terminate prematurely. Examples include syntax errors, accessing undefined variables, or incorrect resource permissions.
- Lambda automatically logs unhandled exceptions in **CloudWatch Logs**.

1. **Example of an Unhandled Exception:**

```python
Copy code
def lambda_handler(event, context):
    # This will cause an unhandled exception
(ZeroDivisionError)
    result = 1 / 0
    return result
```

1. **Timeout Errors:**

- Lambda functions have a maximum execution time (timeout), and if a function exceeds this time, AWS automatically terminates it. Timeout errors typically occur in long-running operations such as large file processing or waiting for an external API.

   1. **Solution:** Always set appropriate timeouts and include logic to handle potential retries or fallbacks when a function might exceed the execution window.
2. **Out of Memory Errors:**

- These errors occur when the Lambda function exceeds its allocated memory. Lambda provides logs that show memory consumption, helping you identify if memory is a problem.

   1. **Solution:** Monitor memory usage via **CloudWatch** and adjust the memory settings as needed.

Setting Up Dead Letter Queues (DLQs)

Dead Letter Queues (DLQs) capture failed Lambda events when the function exhausts all retry attempts. DLQs can help you capture events that fail due to transient errors or unhandled exceptions for later analysis or reprocessing.

1. **How DLQs Work:**

- When a Lambda function fails after the maximum number of retries (for asynchronous invocations) or when synchronous invocations return errors, the event is sent to a Dead Letter Queue (DLQ), such as an **Amazon SQS** queue or an **Amazon SNS** topic.

1. **Setting Up a DLQ:**

- **Step 1:** In the **Lambda Console**, select your function and navigate to the **Asynchronous Invocation** settings.
- **Step 2:** Under **Dead Letter Queue**, select **SQS** or **SNS** and specify the target resource (queue or topic).

1. Alternatively, you can configure a DLQ using the **AWS CLI**:

```bash
Copy code
aws lambda update-function-configuration \
  --function-name MyLambdaFunction \
  --dead-letter-config
  TargetArn=arn:aws:sqs:us-east-1:123456789012:my-queue
```

1. **Consuming Events from DLQs:**

- Once the failed events are in the DLQ, you can consume them using an SQS poller, another Lambda function, or an external system to analyze or reprocess the events.

1. **Best Practices for DLQs:**

- Set up monitoring for DLQs using **CloudWatch** to ensure that failed events are being properly addressed.
- Implement automated retries or alerting systems when DLQ message volumes exceed thresholds, signaling potential issues with your Lambda function.

Using AWS Lambda Destinations for Error Handling

Lambda Destinations offer another way to handle both successful and failed asynchronous invocations. Unlike DLQs, which capture only failed events, Lambda Destinations allow you to route both **success** and **failure**

events to different services such as **SQS, SNS, EventBridge**, or **another Lambda function**.

1. **Types of Lambda Destinations:**

- **Success Destination:** Routes successful event results to a specified service.
- **Failure Destination:** Routes failed events or errors to a specified service.

1. **Setting Up Lambda Destinations:**

- **Step 1:** In the **Lambda Console**, navigate to the **Asynchronous Invocation** settings.
- **Step 2:** Under **Destination settings**, specify the target service for both success and failure events.

1. Alternatively, use the **AWS CLI** to configure destinations:

```bash
Copy code
aws lambda update-event-source-mapping \
  --function-name MyLambdaFunction \
  --destination-config '{"OnFailure":
{"Destination":"arn:aws:sqs:us-east-
1:123456789012:my-queue"}}'
```

1. **Use Case Example:**

- You can use a **Failure Destination** to send failed events to an SNS topic, which in turn can notify the DevOps team about the failure.
- Success events can be sent to an SQS queue for further processing by downstream services.

1. **Comparing DLQs vs Lambda Destinations:**

- **DLQs** are limited to handling only failed invocations and cannot differentiate between error types. **Lambda Destinations**, on the other hand, allow for more flexible routing for both successful and failed invocations.
- For scenarios requiring post-processing of success results or more detailed failure handling, use **Lambda Destinations**.

Best Practices for Fault Tolerance

Building fault-tolerant Lambda functions ensures that your application continues to function correctly even in the event of failures. The following best practices can help:

1. **Idempotency:**

- Ensure your Lambda functions are **idempotent** so that repeated invocations (due to retries) produce the same result. This prevents issues such as duplicating database entries or processing the same event multiple times.
- For example, when writing data to a database, check if the entry already exists before inserting it again.

1. **Use Retries Effectively:**

- AWS automatically retries **asynchronous invocations** (e.g., events from S3, SNS) twice before sending the event to a DLQ or Destination.
- For synchronous invocations (like those triggered by API Gateway), retries are not automatic, so you should implement your retry logic, especially when interacting with third-party services.
- Use **exponential backoff** with retries to reduce the load on downstream services and avoid overwhelming external APIs.

79

1. Timeout Management:

- Always set appropriate timeouts for your Lambda function to avoid running into unexpected timeouts. Start with the lowest possible timeout and increase based on function behavior.
- Use **AWS Step Functions** for long-running tasks, breaking them into smaller, retryable steps rather than handling everything in a single Lambda invocation.

1. Monitor and Alert with CloudWatch:

- Set up **CloudWatch Alarms** to monitor critical Lambda metrics, such as error counts, function timeouts, or throttling events. Create alerts to notify your team when errors exceed thresholds.
- Example: Create an alarm for a high number of function errors over a 5-minute period:

```bash
Copy code
aws cloudwatch put-metric-alarm \
  --alarm-name LambdaErrorAlarm \
  --metric-name Errors \
  --namespace AWS/Lambda \
  --statistic Sum \
  --period 300 \
  --threshold 5 \
  --comparison-operator GreaterThanOrEqualToThreshold \
  --dimensions Name=FunctionName,Value=MyLambdaFunction \
  --evaluation-periods 1 \
  --alarm-actions arn:aws:sns:us-east-
1:123456789012:my-sns-topic
```

1. Graceful Error Handling:

- Always return meaningful error messages from your Lambda function so that downstream services or consumers can interpret the failure correctly.
- Log detailed error information in **CloudWatch Logs** for post-mortem analysis. Use structured logging to make logs easily searchable.

Event-Driven Architectures with Lambda

AWS Lambda is ideal for event-driven architectures, where Lambda functions automatically respond to events from various sources like S3, DynamoDB, SNS, SQS, and more. This architecture allows you to build highly scalable, loosely coupled applications that react to changes in data or user actions in real time.

Event Sources: S3, DynamoDB, SNS, SQS, and More

Lambda functions can be triggered by a wide variety of AWS services, enabling the construction of event-driven workflows. Each event source has its specific use cases and characteristics:

1. **Amazon S3 (Simple Storage Service):**

- **Use Case:** Trigger Lambda functions when objects are created, deleted, or modified in an S3 bucket.
- **Example:** Process and resize images, analyze logs, or extract metadata when files are uploaded to an S3 bucket.
- **Event Type:** s3:ObjectCreated:*, s3:ObjectRemoved:*.

1. **Example Event:**

```json
Copy code
{
  "Records": [
    {
      "eventSource": "aws:s3",
      "s3": {
        "bucket": { "name": "my-bucket" },
        "object": { "key": "file.txt" }
      }
    }
  ]
}
```

1. Amazon DynamoDB Streams:

- **Use Case:** Respond to data changes in a DynamoDB table (inserts, updates, or deletes) via DynamoDB Streams.
- **Example:** Synchronize DynamoDB table changes with other databases, trigger notifications, or perform analytics in real time.
- **Event Type:** Record updates from DynamoDB tables.

1. Example Event:

```json
Copy code
{
  "Records": [
    {
      "eventName": "INSERT",
      "dynamodb": {
        "NewImage": {
          "UserId": { "S": "123" },
          "Name": { "S": "Alice" }
```

```
        }
      }
    }
  ]
}
```

1. Amazon SNS (Simple Notification Service):

- **Use Case:** Invoke Lambda in response to SNS topic notifications. SNS is great for fan-out patterns where multiple services need to react to a single event.
- **Example:** Send an email or SMS when a new order is placed or notify several systems about an important system event.
- **Event Type:** SNS notification events.

1. Example Event:

```json
json
Copy code
{
  "Records": [
    {
      "Sns": {
        "Message": "Order placed: #12345"
      }
    }
  ]
}
```

1. Amazon SQS (Simple Queue Service):

- **Use Case:** Trigger Lambda functions when messages arrive in an SQS queue. SQS ensures reliable delivery of messages between distributed services.

- **Example:** Process work items asynchronously, such as background tasks, order fulfillment, or log processing.
- **Event Type:** SQS messages delivered to the queue.

1. **Example Event:**

```json
Copy code
{
  "Records": [
    {
      "body": "Task to process"
    }
  ]
}
```

1. **Amazon EventBridge (formerly CloudWatch Events):**

- **Use Case:** EventBridge enables event-driven workflows by routing events from various sources (AWS services or custom applications) to Lambda.
- **Example:** Trigger Lambda functions based on system health checks, scheduled events, or any custom event from applications.
- **Event Type:** System and application events.

1. **Example Event:**

```json
Copy code
```

```
{
  "source": "aws.ec2",
  "detail": {
    "state": "running"
  }
}
```

Implementing Event-Driven Workflows

Lambda can act as the core processing unit in complex, event-driven workflows. Here's how to design and implement event-driven workflows using Lambda and AWS services:

1. **Chaining Lambda Functions via Events:**

- **Use Case:** For workflows that require multiple processing steps, you can chain Lambda functions using SNS, SQS, or EventBridge to trigger subsequent functions.
- **Example:** In a data ingestion pipeline, you can use one Lambda function to validate data, another to transform it, and another to store it in a database. Each Lambda function can trigger the next using SNS or SQS.

1. **Implementation:**

- Function 1 writes a message to SNS.
- SNS triggers Function 2, which writes to SQS.
- Function 3 consumes the message from SQS and processes it.

1. **Orchestrating Complex Workflows with Step Functions:**

- **AWS Step Functions** provide a state machine to coordinate multiple Lambda functions in a defined sequence. This is useful for long-running or multi-step processes, handling retries, and conditional logic.
- **Example:** In an order processing system, Step Functions could orchestrate the sequence of Lambda invocations for order validation, payment

processing, and shipping confirmation.

1. **Steps:**

- Use Step Functions to define states, transitions, and error handling.
- Each state invokes a Lambda function and proceeds to the next based on conditions.

1. **Real-Time Data Processing with Streams:**

- For real-time applications, **Kinesis Data Streams** or **DynamoDB Streams** can feed data to Lambda for real-time processing.
- **Example:** Use Lambda to analyze streaming data (e.g., IoT data or social media feeds) as it arrives, and store the results in S3 or DynamoDB for further analysis.

1. **Implementation:**

- Use Kinesis as the event source for Lambda.
- Process batches of streaming data records in Lambda and send results to another service.

Using Lambda as a Backend for Real-Time Applications

AWS Lambda can serve as a scalable backend for real-time applications, handling user requests via API Gateway, processing data in real time, and interacting with databases and other services.

1. **API Gateway + Lambda for Real-Time APIs:**

- **Use Case:** Combine **API Gateway** and Lambda to build RESTful or WebSocket APIs. API Gateway manages HTTP(S) requests, while Lambda functions process the business logic.
- **Example:** A real-time chat application or a real-time stock price tracker

using WebSockets.

1. **Implementation:**

- API Gateway handles incoming HTTP or WebSocket requests and routes them to Lambda.
- Lambda processes the requests (e.g., querying a database, processing data) and returns a response via API Gateway.

1. **Real-Time Notifications with SNS and Lambda:**

- **Use Case:** For real-time notifications, SNS can publish messages to subscribers (e.g., users or other services), and Lambda can act on these messages to process and deliver notifications in real time.
- **Example:** Send an SMS or push notification when a user's order status changes.

1. **Real-Time Data Analysis with Kinesis and Lambda:**

- **Use Case:** Kinesis Data Streams can capture real-time data (e.g., click-streams, sensor data) and trigger Lambda functions to analyze the data.
- **Example:** In an IoT system, Lambda could process sensor data in real time and trigger alerts based on thresholds.

Best Practices for Event Handling in Lambda

1. **Idempotency:**

- Ensure Lambda functions are **idempotent**, meaning repeated executions of the same event should produce the same result. This is especially important when handling retries or failures to avoid duplicate operations (e.g., inserting the same record multiple times).

1. **Error Handling and Retries:**

- Use **dead letter queues (DLQs)** to capture failed event processing and retry logic to ensure fault tolerance.
- For **asynchronous invocations**, Lambda retries events twice before sending them to a DLQ. Implement proper error handling for downstream service failures.

1. **Optimize for Performance:**

- Minimize function cold starts by keeping your function lightweight and using **Provisioned Concurrency** for high-demand functions.
- Tune memory allocation based on the function's workload to optimize for speed and cost-efficiency.

1. **Event Filtering:**

- Use **event filters** to reduce unnecessary invocations. For example, in S3, you can trigger Lambda functions only for specific file types (e.g., .jpg) or paths, reducing execution overhead.

1. **Example: Filtering by File Type in S3**

- Set up an event filter to trigger Lambda only when .jpg files are uploaded, preventing unnecessary invocations for other file types.

1. **Use Batching for High Throughput:**

- For high-volume data sources like Kinesis or DynamoDB Streams, process records in batches to improve efficiency. Configure batch size settings to maximize throughput while keeping execution times manageable.

1. **Example:** Set the BatchSize parameter to process multiple records in a single Lambda invocation:

```bash
Copy code
aws lambda create-event-source-mapping \
  --function-name MyLambdaFunction \
  --batch-size 100 \
  --event-source-arn
  arn:aws:kinesis:us-east-1:123456789012:stream/my-stream
```

1. **Security Best Practices:**

- Use **IAM roles** to grant Lambda the minimum required permissions for accessing other AWS services. Avoid using overly permissive roles.
- Secure event sources, such as using **encryption** for S3 or ensuring **API Gateway** endpoints are protected with IAM roles or **Cognito** for user authentication.

Deploying and Managing Lambda Functions

A WS Lambda offers several powerful tools and techniques for deploying and managing your functions. This includes using AWS SAM for simplified deployment, managing Lambda versions and aliases for better control, implementing blue/green deployments to reduce risk, and integrating Lambda functions into CI/CD pipelines using AWS CodePipeline and CodeBuild.

Using AWS SAM for Deployment

The **AWS Serverless Application Model (SAM)** is an open-source framework designed to simplify the deployment and management of serverless applications. SAM provides a simplified syntax for defining serverless resources such as Lambda functions, API Gateway, DynamoDB, and others.

1. **Installing AWS SAM CLI:**

- Install SAM CLI on your machine using the instructions from the <u>AWS SAM installation guide</u>.

1. Example for macOS:

```bash
Copy code
brew tap aws/tap
brew install aws-sam-cli
```

1. Writing a SAM Template:

- SAM templates are written in YAML format and define the resources needed for your serverless application.
- Here's an example of a basic SAM template to deploy a Lambda function:

1. Example: SAM Template (template.yaml)

```yaml
Copy code
AWSTemplateFormatVersion: '2010-09-09'
Transform: AWS::Serverless-2016-10-31
Resources:
  MyLambdaFunction:
    Type: AWS::Serverless::Function
    Properties:
      Handler: app.lambda_handler
      Runtime: python3.8
      CodeUri: ./src
      Events:
        ApiGateway:
          Type: Api
          Properties:
            Path: /hello
            Method: get
```

1. Building and Deploying the Lambda Function with SAM:

- **Step 1:** Use the sam build command to package the Lambda function and its dependencies:

```bash
Copy code
sam build
```

- **Step 2:** Deploy the Lambda function using sam deploy. This will package your application, upload it to S3, and create a CloudFormation stack:

```bash
Copy code
sam deploy --guided
```

- The —guided option walks you through setting up deployment configurations like the S3 bucket and stack name.

1. **Testing Locally with SAM:**

- You can run your Lambda function locally for testing with the SAM CLI:

```bash
Copy code
sam local invoke "MyLambdaFunction"
```

- You can also run the entire application locally with:

```bash
bash
Copy code
sam local start-api
```

1. **Monitoring and Managing Resources:**

- Once deployed, SAM uses **AWS CloudFormation** to manage the Lambda function and other resources. Changes to the template can be deployed via CloudFormation updates.

Managing Lambda Versions and Aliases

Lambda **versions** and **aliases** help manage different deployments of a Lambda function and route traffic to specific versions.

1. **Lambda Versions:**

- Each time you deploy an updated Lambda function, you can **publish** a version. Versions are immutable snapshots of your function code and configuration.

1. **Example: Publishing a New Version**

```bash
bash
Copy code
aws lambda publish-version --function-name MyLambdaFunction
```

- Versions are numbered starting from 1 and are immutable once created, ensuring that the specific function version cannot change.

1. Lambda Aliases:

- Aliases allow you to create pointers to specific function versions, making it easier to route traffic between different versions (e.g., dev, prod, test).
- An alias can be updated to point to a new version without changing the function name or the client-facing endpoint.

1. Example: Creating and Updating Aliases

- Create an alias for version 2:

```bash
Copy code
aws lambda create-alias \
   --function-name MyLambdaFunction \
   --name prod \
   --function-version 2
```

- Update the alias to point to a newer version:

```bash
Copy code
aws lambda update-alias \
   --function-name MyLambdaFunction \
   --name prod \
   --function-version 3
```

1. Weighted Aliases for Canary Releases:

- You can use **weighted aliases** to route a percentage of traffic to a new version, facilitating gradual rollouts.

1. **Example:**

```bash
bash
Copy code
aws lambda update-alias \
   --function-name MyLambdaFunction \
   --name prod \
   --routing-config
'{"AdditionalVersionWeights": {"3": 0.1}}'
```

- This routes 90% of traffic to version 2 and 10% to version 3, allowing for testing with real traffic before full deployment.

Implementing Blue/Green Deployments

Blue/Green Deployments reduce the risk of deployment failures by gradually shifting traffic from one version of a Lambda function (blue) to a new version (green). If the new version has issues, you can easily roll back without affecting users.

1. **Steps for Blue/Green Deployment:**

- **Step 1:** Create a new version of the Lambda function (green version) and test it thoroughly.
- **Step 2:** Create or update an alias (e.g., prod) to point to the new version.
- **Step 3:** Gradually shift traffic from the blue (old) version to the green version by using **weighted aliases**.

1. **Routing Traffic with Weighted Aliases:**

- You can route a small percentage of traffic to the new version and gradually increase it as confidence in the new version grows. If issues are detected, you can quickly revert to the old version by updating the alias.

1. **Monitoring During Deployment:**

- Use **Amazon CloudWatch** to monitor metrics such as latency, error rates, and throttling for both versions. If any issues are detected with the green version, traffic can be shifted back to the blue version immediately.

1. **Example: Reverting Traffic to Blue Version:**

```bash
Copy code
aws lambda update-alias \
  --function-name MyLambdaFunction \
  --name prod \
  --routing-config '
{"AdditionalVersionWeights": {"2": 1.0}}'
```

CI/CD Pipeline Integration with AWS CodePipeline and CodeBuild

Automating deployments using a **CI/CD pipeline** ensures that new Lambda function versions are tested, built, and deployed efficiently. **AWS CodePipeline** and **AWS CodeBuild** are fully managed services that help automate the build and deployment process for Lambda.

1. **Setting Up AWS CodePipeline:**

- **CodePipeline** automates the process of building, testing, and deploying Lambda functions. It integrates with GitHub, Bitbucket, or AWS CodeCommit as a source.

Serverless Frameworks and Tools for Python Development

When building serverless applications in Python, several frameworks and tools streamline development, deployment, and management of AWS Lambda functions. These tools abstract much of the complexity of AWS infrastructure and provide a simpler, more efficient way to develop serverless applications. Below is an overview of the most popular serverless frameworks for Python development, including **Serverless Framework**, **Zappa**, and **Chalice**, along with a comparison of their features.

Overview of the Serverless Framework

The **Serverless Framework** is a popular open-source framework that simplifies the development and deployment of serverless applications across multiple cloud providers, including AWS, Azure, Google Cloud, and more. For AWS Lambda and Python, it provides a structured way to define functions, event sources, and resources.

1. **Key Features:**

- **Multi-cloud support**: The Serverless Framework works across AWS, Azure, Google Cloud, and others, offering flexibility.
- **Declarative YAML configuration**: Resources and functions are defined

in a serverless.yml file, making it easy to configure and deploy.

- **Built-in integration with AWS services**: The framework natively supports event triggers like S3, API Gateway, DynamoDB, SQS, SNS, and others.
- **Plugins**: A large ecosystem of plugins extends the functionality, including support for WebSockets, Step Functions, and more.

1. **Basic Setup:**

- First, install the framework globally:

```bash
Copy code
npm install -g serverless
```

- Create a new Python project:

```bash
Copy code
serverless create --template aws-python3 --path my-service
cd my-service
```

1. **Defining a Serverless Application (serverless.yml):**

- The serverless.yml file is used to define the functions and event sources that trigger them.

1. **Example: Basic serverless.yml Configuration:**

```yaml
yaml
Copy code
service: my-python-service
provider:
  name: aws
  runtime: python3.8

functions:
  hello:
    handler: handler.hello
    events:
      - http:
          path: hello
          method: get

resources:
  Resources:
    MyS3Bucket:
      Type: AWS::S3::Bucket
      Properties:
        BucketName: my-python-bucket
```

1. **Deploying the Application:**

• Deploy your service with the following command:

```bash
bash
Copy code
serverless deploy
```

1. **Monitoring and Management:**

• Serverless Framework offers an integrated dashboard for monitoring, debugging, and managing your deployed Lambda functions in real-time.

1. **Pros:**

- Multi-cloud support.
- Large community and extensive plugin ecosystem.
- Well-documented and easy-to-use.

1. **Cons:**

- The serverless.yml file can get complex for larger applications.
- Overhead in managing dependencies and plugins for multi-cloud support.

Using Zappa for Python Applications

Zappa is another popular Python-focused serverless framework that simplifies the deployment of **Python WSGI** applications to AWS Lambda and API Gateway. Zappa is particularly suited for deploying traditional Python web applications such as **Flask, Django**, or **Pyramid**.

1. **Key Features:**

- **WSGI application support**: Zappa makes it easy to deploy Python WSGI-compatible apps (Flask, Django) to AWS Lambda.
- **Zero-config deployments**: With minimal configuration, Zappa can handle the complexities of packaging, deploying, and managing serverless Python apps.
- **Auto-scaling**: Since the app is deployed on Lambda, Zappa leverages Lambda's auto-scaling capabilities automatically.

1. **Basic Setup:**

- Install Zappa using pip:

```bash
Copy code
pip install zappa
```

- Initialize Zappa in your project directory:

```bash
Copy code
zappa init
```

- During initialization, Zappa will ask for information like the name of the app, the AWS region, and whether to deploy to a staging environment.

1. **Deploying a Zappa Application:**

- To deploy your application, simply run:

```bash
Copy code
zappa deploy
```

- Zappa will handle packaging, uploading, and configuring the AWS infrastructure (API Gateway, Lambda, etc.) automatically.

1. **Example for Flask:**

- If you're using **Flask**, Zappa can be configured with minimal changes:

1. **Example: Basic Flask Application (app.py):**

```python
Copy code
from flask import Flask

app = Flask(__name__)

@app.route('/')
def hello():
    return "Hello, World!"

if __name__ == "__main__":
    app.run()
```

- Once your Flask app is ready, run zappa deploy to deploy it as a serverless app on AWS.

1. **Managing and Updating the App:**

- To update your application after making changes:

```bash
Copy code
zappa update
```

1. **Pros:**

- Simplifies deploying existing Python web frameworks like Flask and Django.
- Zero-config, easy setup for Python developers.

103

- Auto-manages API Gateway and Lambda configuration.

1. **Cons:**

- Primarily designed for WSGI apps, which may not be ideal for non-web use cases.
- Some limitations in terms of scaling for high-throughput applications.

Building with AWS Chalice

AWS Chalice is a Python-only framework developed by AWS specifically for building serverless applications that use AWS Lambda and API Gateway. Chalice focuses on ease of use and simplicity, offering a Pythonic way to define APIs, event-driven applications, and deploy them on AWS.

1. **Key Features:**

- **AWS-native**: Deep integration with AWS services, including S3, DynamoDB, SNS, and SQS.
- **Python-first design**: Chalice is designed specifically for Python developers and offers a very straightforward experience.
- **Automatic routing with API Gateway**: Chalice makes it easy to define and manage REST APIs with API Gateway.

1. **Basic Setup:**

- Install AWS Chalice:

```bash
Copy code
pip install chalice
```

- Create a new project:

```bash
Copy code
chalice new-project myproject
cd myproject
```

1. **Example Chalice Application:**

- A simple Chalice app with one route might look like this:

1. **Example: app.py**

```python
Copy code
from chalice import Chalice

app = Chalice(app_name='myapp')

@app.route('/')
def index():
    return {'hello': 'world'}
```

1. **Deploying with Chalice:**

- Deploying the app to AWS:

```bash
Copy code
chalice deploy
```

- Chalice will automatically package the code, configure API Gateway, and deploy the Lambda function.

1. **Integrating with AWS Services:**

- Chalice integrates seamlessly with AWS services. For example, to trigger a Lambda function when a new object is uploaded to S3:

1. **Example:**

```python
Copy code
@app.on_s3_event(bucket='mybucket')
def handler(event):
    print(f"New object uploaded: {event.key}")
```

1. **Pros:**

- AWS-native and designed specifically for Python developers.
- Simple syntax and rapid deployment of serverless applications.
- Deep integration with AWS services.

1. **Cons:**

- Limited to AWS Lambda and API Gateway (no multi-cloud support).
- Smaller community compared to Serverless Framework.

Comparing Different Serverless Frameworks
Feature**Serverless FrameworkZappaAWS Chalice**
Cloud Provider Support
Multi-cloud (AWS, Azure, GCP)
AWS Only

AWS Only
Primary Use Case
General serverless development
WSGI apps (Flask, Django)
Python APIs and event-driven
Complexity
Moderate (YAML config)
Simple (minimal config)
Simple (Pythonic syntax)
Deployment Management
CLI-based with plugins
Fully automated via CLI
AWS-native with Chalice CLI
Multi-Service Support
Extensive (S3, DynamoDB, etc.)
Focus on API Gateway/Lambda
Excellent AWS service support
Cold Start Mitigation
Requires external handling
Managed by AWS
Managed by AWS
Plugin Ecosystem
Large and growing
Limited
AWS-focused
Summary:

- **Serverless Framework** is the most flexible and multi-cloud-friendly framework with a large community, making it a good choice for large-scale, multi-cloud serverless projects.
- **Zappa** is ideal for Python developers who need to quickly deploy existing web applications like Flask or Django to AWS Lambda.
- **AWS Chalice** is a great choice for Python developers who want a

tightly integrated, AWS-native solution for building APIs or event-driven architectures with minimal setup and straightforward syntax.

Use Cases and Real-World Examples of AWS Lambda

AWS Lambda's flexibility and scalability make it ideal for a wide variety of use cases. Below are examples of how Lambda can be leveraged for building RESTful APIs, serverless ETL pipelines, real-time data processing, and automating infrastructure tasks.

1. Building a RESTful API with Lambda and API Gateway

Use Case: A common scenario is creating a **serverless REST API** using **AWS Lambda** and **API Gateway**. This eliminates the need for traditional server infrastructure, allowing the API to scale automatically with user demand. For example, you could build a product catalog API that handles product creation, updates, and queries.

Real-World Example: Imagine you need to build a RESTful API for an e-commerce platform where users can retrieve product details, add new products, and update existing ones. Each API request would trigger a Lambda function to interact with the data store (DynamoDB or RDS).

Steps to Build the API:

1. **Set up API Gateway:**

- API Gateway will act as the frontend, routing incoming HTTP requests to Lambda functions.
- Define RESTful endpoints like /products, /products/{id}, using API Gateway.

1. **Create Lambda Functions:**

- Each Lambda function will correspond to a specific API endpoint (GET, POST, PUT, DELETE).
- Use **DynamoDB** or **RDS** to store product data.

1. **Example Lambda Function for Fetching Product Data:**

```python
Copy code
import json
import boto3

dynamodb = boto3.resource('dynamodb')
table = dynamodb.Table('Products')

def lambda_handler(event, context):
    product_id = event['pathParameters']['id']
    response = table.get_item(Key={'id': product_id})
    return {
        'statusCode': 200,
        'body': json.dumps(response['Item'])
    }
```

1. **Deploy and Test:**

- Deploy the API Gateway and Lambda function, then test your API endpoints.

Benefits:

- **Auto-scaling:** Automatically handles millions of requests without manual intervention.
- **Cost-efficiency:** You only pay for the compute time that Lambda functions use, avoiding costs associated with idle infrastructure.
- **Maintenance-free:** No need to manage servers, software updates, or scaling.

2. Serverless ETL Pipelines with Lambda and S3

Use Case: Serverless **ETL (Extract, Transform, Load)** pipelines are used to process and transform data in real time or batches. AWS Lambda, combined with **Amazon S3** and **AWS Glue**, is an ideal solution for serverless ETL tasks such as cleaning, transforming, and loading large datasets into a data lake or data warehouse.

Real-World Example: Consider a use case where raw log files are uploaded to an S3 bucket, and each file needs to be processed (e.g., data normalization, filtering, aggregation). Lambda functions can be triggered automatically whenever new files are uploaded to S3, process the data, and store the cleaned results back in S3 or a database (e.g., Redshift).

Steps to Build the ETL Pipeline:

1. **S3 Trigger:**

- Set up an S3 bucket to trigger Lambda functions when new files are uploaded.
- This can be configured through S3's event notifications, which automatically invoke Lambda when a file is added or modified.

1. **Lambda Function to Process the File:**

- The Lambda function will read the S3 file, perform the necessary transformations, and store the result back in S3 or another service.

1. **Example Lambda Function for Processing S3 File:**

```python
Copy code
import json
import boto3
import csv

s3 = boto3.client('s3')

def lambda_handler(event, context):
    # Get the S3 bucket and object key from the event
    bucket = event['Records'][0]['s3']['bucket']['name']
    key = event['Records'][0]['s3']['object']['key']

    # Download the file
    file_obj = s3.get_object(Bucket=bucket, Key=key)
    file_content =
    file_obj['Body'].read().decode('utf-8').splitlines()

    # Process the file (e.g., convert to CSV)
    reader = csv.reader(file_content)
    processed_data = [row for row in reader if len(row) > 1]

    # Upload the processed data back to S3 or another service
    s3.put_object(Bucket='processed-bucket', Key=key,
    Body=json.dumps(processed_data))

    return {
        'statusCode': 200,
        'body': 'File processed successfully'
    }
```

1. **Extend the Pipeline with AWS Glue:**

- Use **AWS Glue** to catalog and manage metadata for the processed files.
- Glue can also be used to perform complex transformations before loading data into data warehouses like **Amazon Redshift**.

Benefits:

- **Serverless scalability:** Automatically handles varying file sizes and loads without manual scaling.
- **Low cost:** You only pay for the Lambda invocations and compute time used during data processing.
- **Real-time processing:** Lambda can process files as soon as they are uploaded, making it perfect for real-time analytics.

3. Real-Time Data Processing with Lambda and Kinesis

Use Case: AWS Lambda can process real-time data streams from sources like **Amazon Kinesis** or **DynamoDB Streams**. This is ideal for use cases like real-time analytics, monitoring, log analysis, and Internet of Things (IoT) applications.

Real-World Example: Suppose you have a stock trading platform that needs to process a real-time stream of stock trades. AWS Lambda, combined with **Amazon Kinesis Data Streams**, can process this data in real time, compute aggregate metrics, and push the results to **Amazon Redshift** or S3 for analysis.

Steps to Build Real-Time Data Processing:

1. **Set Up Kinesis Data Stream:**

- Create a Kinesis data stream to collect incoming stock trade data in real time.
- Stream shards can be configured based on the volume of incoming data.

1. **Create Lambda Function to Process Stream Data:**

- Lambda will be triggered by the Kinesis stream and process incoming records in batches.

1. **Example Lambda Function for Processing Kinesis Data:**

```python
Copy code
import json

def lambda_handler(event, context):
    for record in event['Records']:
        # Decode the Kinesis data
        data = json.loads(record['kinesis']['data'])

        # Process the stock trade (e.g., calculate averages)
        print(f"Processing trade for stock:
 {data['stock_symbol']} at price: {data['price']}")

    return {
        'statusCode': 200,
        'body': 'Trade data processed successfully'
    }
```

1. **Deploy and Monitor:**

- Deploy the Lambda function, and it will automatically process data from Kinesis in near real-time.
- Use **Amazon CloudWatch** to monitor the processing performance and scaling behavior.

Benefits:

- **Real-time insights:** Lambda processes data as it arrives, allowing for near-instant analytics or actions.

- **Scalability:** Kinesis and Lambda scale automatically based on the incoming data stream volume.
- **Cost-effective:** Only pay for the processing time, with no need to manage servers.

4. Automating Infrastructure Tasks with Lambda

Use Case: AWS Lambda is highly effective for automating common infrastructure tasks such as scaling EC2 instances, cleaning up unused resources, rotating secrets, and more. These functions are often triggered by events from services like **CloudWatch, SNS,** or **EventBridge**.

Real-World Example: Suppose you need to automate the process of **scaling EC2 instances** during peak load periods and scaling them back down when traffic reduces. Lambda can monitor system metrics and automatically trigger actions based on defined thresholds.

Steps to Automate Infrastructure Tasks:

1. **Trigger Lambda via CloudWatch Events:**

- Use **CloudWatch Alarms** or **EventBridge** to trigger a Lambda function when EC2 instance CPU usage exceeds a certain threshold.

1. **Create Lambda Function to Scale EC2 Instances:**

- The Lambda function will use **Boto3** (AWS SDK) to interact with EC2 and either start or stop instances based on the alarm condition.

1. **Example Lambda Function to Scale EC2 Instances:**

```
python
Copy code
```

115

```
import boto3

ec2 = boto3.client('ec2')

def lambda_handler(event, context):
    # Scale up logic (e.g., start EC2 instances)
    response =
    ec2.start_instances(InstanceIds=['i-1234567890abcdef'])
    print(f'Started EC2 instances: {response}')

    return {
        'statusCode': 200,
        'body': 'EC2 instances started successfully'
    }
```

1. **Monitor and React:**

- CloudWatch can trigger this Lambda function when specific metrics, such as CPU usage, exceed thresholds.
- Lambda will execute the scaling action in response to the event.

Benefits:

- **Automation:** Lambda automates manual tasks like resource scaling, reducing the need for human intervention.
- **Cost-efficiency:** Automating tasks such as cleaning up idle resources can help save costs.
- **Flexibility:** Lambda can be used to trigger actions across a wide range of AWS services and infrastructure components.

Troubleshooting and Debugging in AWS Lambda

D ebugging and troubleshooting AWS Lambda functions can be challenging due to their ephemeral nature and distributed architecture. However, understanding common issues, leveraging CloudWatch for logging, and implementing effective strategies can significantly ease the process. Below are strategies for addressing common issues, debugging techniques, and methods for handling errors in complex workflows.

Common Issues in Python Lambda Functions

1. **Cold Start Latency:**

- **Description:** Cold starts occur when a new instance of a Lambda function is initialized, leading to increased latency for the first request.
- **Solution:** Use **Provisioned Concurrency** to keep a number of instances warm and ready to handle requests.

1. **Timeout Errors:**

- **Description:** If a Lambda function takes longer than its configured timeout (maximum 15 minutes), it will be forcibly terminated, resulting in a timeout error.

- **Solution:** Analyze the function's performance, optimize the code, and increase the timeout if necessary. Ensure that any blocking operations (like external API calls) are managed appropriately.

1. **Memory Errors:**

- **Description:** Lambda functions have a memory limit, and exceeding this limit results in a memory error.
- **Solution:** Monitor memory usage via CloudWatch metrics. Optimize the code to use memory more efficiently or increase the memory allocation for the function.

1. **Permission Issues:**

- **Description:** Functions may fail to access required AWS services due to incorrect IAM role permissions.
- **Solution:** Ensure that the Lambda function's execution role has the correct permissions to access necessary resources (e.g., S3, DynamoDB).

1. **Dependency Issues:**

- **Description:** Errors due to missing or incompatible package dependencies can occur if the deployment package is not set up correctly.
- **Solution:** Ensure all dependencies are included in the deployment package or use Lambda Layers to manage dependencies efficiently.

Strategies for Debugging with CloudWatch Logs

AWS CloudWatch Logs are the primary tool for troubleshooting and debugging Lambda functions. Here's how to effectively use CloudWatch for debugging:

1. **Enable Logging:**

- Ensure that logging is enabled in your Lambda function. Use Python's built-in logging library to log important events, errors, and variables.

1. **Example: Basic Logging in a Lambda Function:**

```python
python
Copy code
import logging

logger = logging.getLogger()
logger.setLevel(logging.INFO)

def lambda_handler(event, context):
    logger.info("Received event: %s", event)
    # Your logic here
    return {"statusCode": 200}
```

1. **Monitor CloudWatch Logs:**

- Navigate to the **CloudWatch Console** to view logs for your Lambda function. Each invocation generates a log stream where you can see the output from your logging statements.
- Look for patterns in the logs that indicate the source of issues, such as recurring errors or performance bottlenecks.

1. **Structured Logging:**

- Use structured logging to make logs easier to search and analyze. For example, log messages in JSON format with relevant metadata (like request IDs, user IDs, and timestamps).

1. **Example: Structured Logging:**

```python
python
Copy code
import json

def lambda_handler(event, context):
    log_data = {
        "event": event,
        "context": {
            "function_name": context.function_name,
            "aws_request_id": context.aws_request_id,
        }
    }
    logger.info(json.dumps(log_data))
    return {"statusCode": 200}
```

1. **Log Metrics for Performance:**

- Log performance metrics such as execution duration, memory usage, and error counts. This helps identify potential performance issues or bottlenecks in your code.

Fixing Memory and Timeout Issues

Addressing memory and timeout issues is crucial for ensuring Lambda functions run smoothly. Here are strategies to handle these issues:

1. **Monitor Resource Usage:**

- Use CloudWatch metrics to monitor memory usage and execution duration. Identify patterns that may indicate the need for adjustments.
- Look for metrics such as MaxMemoryUsed and Duration in the Cloud-Watch console for your Lambda function.

1. **Adjust Memory Settings:**

- Lambda allows you to adjust memory allocation from 128 MB to 10,240 MB. Increasing memory not only provides more RAM but also allocates more CPU power, potentially speeding up execution.
- **Example: Adjusting Memory via AWS CLI:**

```bash
Copy code
aws lambda update-function-configuration --function-name
MyLambdaFunction --memory-size 1024  # Set to 1GB
```

1. **Optimize Code:**

- Review the code for performance inefficiencies, such as blocking operations, excessive loops, or inefficient data structures.
- Profile the function using tools like **AWS X-Ray** to identify bottlenecks and optimize code accordingly.

1. **Use Asynchronous Calls:**

- For external API calls or long-running tasks, consider using asynchronous requests (e.g., using asyncio or threads) to avoid blocking the main execution flow, which can lead to timeouts.

1. **Implement Efficient Logic:**

- Break down complex tasks into smaller Lambda functions or use AWS Step Functions for orchestration. This can prevent individual functions from exceeding time limits.

Handling Errors in Complex Workflows

Complex workflows, especially those involving multiple Lambda functions or other AWS services, can introduce unique challenges in error handling.

Here's how to effectively manage errors in such scenarios:

1. Implement Retry Logic:

- Use built-in retries for asynchronous invocations, which automatically retry failed executions. For synchronous invocations, implement custom retry logic in your application.

1. Use AWS Step Functions:

- For complex workflows, consider using **AWS Step Functions** to orchestrate multiple Lambda functions. Step Functions provide built-in error handling, retries, and state management.
- You can define workflows that specify what to do in case of failure, including retries or directing the flow to error handling states.

1. Dead Letter Queues (DLQs):

- For asynchronous invocations, configure Dead Letter Queues to capture failed events. This allows for further analysis and manual processing of events that could not be successfully handled.

1. Example: Configuring a DLQ:

```bash
Copy code
aws lambda update-function-configuration \
  --function-name MyLambdaFunction \
  --dead-letter-config
  TargetArn=arn:aws:sqs:us-east-1:123456789012:my-dlq
```

1. Error Handling in Lambda Functions:

- Implement error handling in your Lambda functions using try-except blocks to catch specific exceptions and return meaningful error messages or take corrective actions.

1. **Example: Error Handling in Lambda:**

```python
Copy code
def lambda_handler(event, context):
    try:
        # Your function logic here
        result = perform_action(event)
        return {"statusCode": 200, "body": result}
    except SpecificError as e:
        logger.error("Handled error: %s", e)
        return {"statusCode": 400, "body": str(e)}
    except Exception as e:
        logger.error("Unhandled error: %s", e)
        return {"statusCode": 500, "body":
"Internal Server Error"}
```

1. **Logging and Monitoring:**

- Continuously log errors and important events to CloudWatch. Use CloudWatch Alarms to monitor for error spikes and automatically notify your team when issues arise.

Future Trends and Developments in Serverless Python

As serverless computing continues to evolve, several trends and advancements are shaping the future of serverless architectures, particularly for Python developers. Understanding these trends will help developers leverage new capabilities, optimize their applications, and remain competitive in the cloud landscape.

Emerging Trends in Serverless Architecture

1. **Increased Adoption of Event-Driven Architectures:**

- Organizations are increasingly adopting event-driven architectures that enable real-time processing of data streams. This trend emphasizes the importance of services like AWS Lambda in building reactive applications that respond to events from various sources such as IoT devices, APIs, and user interactions.

1. **Greater Integration of AI and Machine Learning:**

- The integration of AI and machine learning models into serverless applications is becoming more common. Tools like AWS Lambda enable developers to run ML inference at scale without worrying about infrastructure management. For instance, models can be served via Lambda functions, processing user inputs in real time.

1. **Serverless Security and Compliance:**

- As serverless adoption grows, so does the focus on security and compliance. Companies are implementing more robust security practices tailored for serverless environments, including identity and access management, automated security checks, and monitoring tools designed to catch vulnerabilities specific to serverless architectures.

1. **Multi-Cloud Strategies:**

- Organizations are adopting multi-cloud strategies to avoid vendor lock-in and enhance resilience. Serverless frameworks that support multiple cloud providers (like Serverless Framework) allow developers to deploy applications across AWS, Azure, and Google Cloud, leveraging the strengths of each platform.

1. **Improved Monitoring and Observability:**

- The demand for better observability and monitoring tools is rising. Developers are seeking comprehensive tools that provide insights into the performance and behavior of serverless applications, such as tracing, logging, and alerting mechanisms that allow for proactive troubleshooting.

Upcoming Features in AWS Lambda

1. **Support for Additional Languages:**

- AWS Lambda continues to expand support for programming languages. While Python is already supported, future releases may introduce new runtimes or enhancements to existing ones, allowing developers to leverage the latest language features and libraries.

1. **Improved Provisioned Concurrency:**

- Enhancements to **Provisioned Concurrency** are anticipated, making it easier for developers to manage cold starts and ensure that critical functions are always ready to handle requests with minimal latency.

1. **Integration with New AWS Services:**

- AWS frequently releases new services and features. Lambda is expected to continue evolving alongside these services, enabling tighter integration with offerings like **Amazon EventBridge**, **AWS Glue**, and **Amazon SageMaker** for ML applications.

1. **Increased Event Source Integrations:**

- Future updates may provide support for more event sources, allowing Lambda to respond to an even broader range of events, from more AWS services to third-party applications and APIs.

1. **Enhanced Performance Metrics:**

- AWS is likely to improve the performance metrics available for Lambda functions, enabling more granular insights into function execution, memory consumption, and invocation patterns.

The Future of Python in Cloud Computing

1. **Python as the Language of Choice for Data Science:**

- Python's popularity in data science and machine learning continues to grow, making it a key language in cloud computing environments. The integration of serverless architectures with data science tools allows data scientists to deploy models rapidly and at scale.

1. **Growing Community and Ecosystem:**

- The Python community is vibrant and continues to grow, with numerous libraries and frameworks being developed to simplify serverless application development. This includes libraries for serverless frameworks like **Zappa** and **Chalice** that specifically cater to Python developers.

1. **Interoperability with Other Languages:**

- As cloud platforms evolve, interoperability between Python and other programming languages will become more common. This will allow teams to leverage the strengths of various languages within the same serverless application, promoting collaboration and efficiency.

1. **Enhancements in Asynchronous Programming:**

- The adoption of asynchronous programming in Python (with async and await) will likely increase, allowing developers to write non-blocking code for I/O-bound operations. This can significantly enhance the performance of serverless applications, especially those that rely on external API calls.

Serverless vs Containerized Architectures

1. **Definition and Use Cases:**

- **Serverless Architecture** (like AWS Lambda) abstracts away the underlying infrastructure, allowing developers to focus solely on code. It is ideal for event-driven applications, microservices, and APIs.

- **Containerized Architecture** (using services like AWS ECS or EKS) involves deploying applications in containers, providing more control over the environment and dependencies. It's suited for complex applications requiring specific configurations or a longer execution time.

1. **Scalability:**

- **Serverless:** Automatically scales based on the number of requests. Developers don't need to manage scaling, but there may be limits on concurrency.
- **Containers:** Scaling is managed at the orchestration level. Developers can define how many instances to run, offering more control but requiring more management.

1. **Cold Start vs. Startup Time:**

- **Serverless:** Can experience cold starts, introducing latency for infrequently accessed functions.
- **Containers:** May have longer startup times, but once running, they typically perform consistently without the cold start issue.

1. **Development and Deployment Complexity:**

- **Serverless:** Offers simplicity in deployment and management with a focus on code. However, debugging can be more challenging due to the ephemeral nature of functions.
- **Containers:** Provide more control over the environment and dependencies but require a more complex setup and management process.

1. **Cost Considerations:**

- **Serverless:** Pay-per-use pricing model can lead to cost savings for sporadic workloads, but costs can increase with high usage.

- **Containers:** Typically involve fixed costs based on resources allocated, which may be more predictable but can lead to higher costs if resources are underutilized.

1. **Use Case Suitability:**

- **Serverless** is ideal for lightweight, event-driven applications, while **containerized architectures** are better suited for complex applications that require specific runtime environments, persistent states, or long-running processes.

Conclusion and Next Steps

As serverless computing continues to gain traction, AWS Lambda offers a powerful platform for building scalable, efficient, and cost-effective applications. By leveraging Lambda's capabilities, Python developers can create a variety of applications ranging from APIs to data processing workflows and more. Below is a recap of key concepts, potential next steps, and resources for further learning.

Recap of Key Concepts

1. **Serverless Architecture:**

- Serverless computing allows developers to build and run applications without managing infrastructure. AWS Lambda automatically scales based on demand, enabling efficient resource utilization.

1. **AWS Lambda:**

- A serverless compute service that executes code in response to events. It supports multiple languages, including Python, and is integrated with various AWS services like S3, DynamoDB, SNS, and Kinesis.

1. **Development Frameworks:**

- Frameworks like **Serverless Framework**, **Zappa**, and **AWS Chalice** simplify the deployment and management of serverless applications, each with its strengths and ideal use cases.

1. **Event-Driven Architecture:**

- Lambda's ability to react to events makes it suitable for real-time applications, ETL processes, and microservices. Event sources like S3, API Gateway, and Kinesis enable powerful event-driven workflows.

1. **Debugging and Troubleshooting:**

- CloudWatch Logs and AWS X-Ray are essential tools for monitoring and debugging Lambda functions. Best practices for error handling, optimizing performance, and managing resources can enhance application reliability.

1. **Future Trends:**

- Emerging trends such as enhanced AI integration, event-driven architectures, and the need for robust security and observability are shaping the future of serverless computing and Python development.

Exploring Other AWS Services for Serverless Applications

As you deepen your understanding of serverless architectures, consider exploring complementary AWS services that enhance serverless applications:

- **Amazon API Gateway:** To create, publish, and manage APIs for your Lambda functions.
- **AWS Step Functions:** For orchestrating complex workflows that involve multiple Lambda functions and services.
- **Amazon S3:** For storing data, such as files and logs, that can trigger Lambda functions.

- **Amazon DynamoDB:** A NoSQL database service that integrates seamlessly with Lambda for real-time data processing.
- **Amazon EventBridge:** For building event-driven applications that respond to events from AWS services and external sources.

Expanding to Multi-Cloud Serverless Architectures

As organizations look to avoid vendor lock-in and leverage the strengths of multiple cloud providers, consider the following:

- **Multi-Cloud Strategy:** Research frameworks and tools that support multi-cloud deployments, allowing you to build serverless applications across AWS, Azure, Google Cloud, and more.
- **Interoperability:** Explore ways to integrate services from different cloud providers, such as using APIs or event-driven architectures to facilitate communication between serverless functions across clouds.
- **Cost Management:** Understand the pricing models of different cloud providers to optimize costs and resource utilization in a multi-cloud environment.

Resources for Further Learning

To continue your journey in serverless computing and Python development, explore the following resources:

1. **AWS Documentation:**

- AWS Lambda Documentation
- AWS Serverless Application Model (SAM) Documentation

1. **Online Courses:**

- Platforms like **Coursera, Udemy**, and **Pluralsight** offer courses focused on AWS Lambda and serverless architectures.
- Look for specific courses on Python development in serverless contexts.

1. **Books:**

- "Serverless Architectures on AWS" by Peter Sbarski
- "Python Serverless Microservices" by Mohamed Sarrar

1. **Community and Forums:**

- Join communities such as **AWS Developer Forums, Stack Overflow,** or **Reddit** to connect with other developers and learn from their experiences.
- Attend local meetups or online webinars to network with other professionals and gain insights into current trends.

1. **Blogs and Tutorials:**

- Follow blogs like the **AWS Architecture Blog** or **Serverless.com Blog** for the latest updates, tutorials, and best practices in serverless computing.